THE PREVAILING SOUTH

THE PREVAILING SOUTH

Life & Politics in a Changing Culture

Edited by Dudley Clendinen

LONGSTREET PRESS, INC.
Atlanta, Georgia

Printed in the United States of America

First Printing, 1988

Library of Congress Catalog Card Number 88-081798

ISBN 0-929264-01-0

Design by Paulette Lambert

Published by
LONGSTREET PRESS, INC.
2150 Newmarket Parkway
Suite 102
Marietta, Georgia 30067

Contents

Bill Kovach, the editor of *The Atlanta Journal* and *The Atlanta Constitution,* is a native Southerner and a passionate student of the region's history. Born in Greeneville, Tennessee, in September 1932, and schooled at East Tennessee State University, he has followed the evolution of the South closely, as reporter and editor, for almost thirty years. He covered Appalachia, the civil rights movement and Southern politics for the *Nashville Tennessean* in the sixties, and later, as deputy national editor and then Washington bureau chief of *The New York Times* in the seventies and eighties, he directed coverage of the region and its role in national affairs. Mr. Kovach won a journalism fellowship to Stanford University before joining the *Times* in 1968, and he serves on the Distinguished Advisory Committee of American University in Washington, D.C., and on the Board of Visitors of the Neiman Fellowship Program at Harvard University. He is currently the chairman of the International Communications Committee of the American Society of Newspaper Editors, and he has contributed to two books, *Assignment America,* published by Quadrangle Press in 1974, and *The Art of Writing Non-Fiction,* published by Syracuse Press in 1986. He has been editor of the *The Atlanta Journal* and *The Atlanta Constitution* since the end of 1986, and conceived of this collection as an examination of the state of the South when both major political parties chose it as the site of their 1988 conventions.

Foreword

*J*uly 1864: General Sherman's troops cross the Chattahoochee River and Atlanta is under siege. September 1: Sherman sits upon his horse on a knoll and watches the defeated city burn.

The years since have been years of protracted struggle as the region has sought to digest defeat of dimensions we are only now beginning to truly understand. For the Civil War was a revolution. To accept the terms of defeat meant the region had to rebuild its economy to an alien blueprint and to reshape its society in a manner acceptable to the new vision of the United States that the revolution produced.

Thus the South was thrust into a period of change from which it has yet to emerge. But as a doctor's prescription is often difficult to swallow, so too a victor's terms. For each Southerner who accepted the terms of re-union, there was another whose angry shout of "Never" echoes down the generations. For each Southerner who sought distraction in enterprise and building, there was another who found the Balm of Gilead. For each Southerner who looked with anticipation to the future to be built, there was another who searched the eyes in faded family pictures for the strength to endure. For each white Southerner who moved with ease over the course of the new society, there was a black who met strange obstacles that at times proved deadly snares to the feet.

Springing as they did from the same source, these Southern impulses were like tributaries of a stream. Each arising on the same watershed, but mingling and confusing themselves in the riverbed, they struggled to control the course. First one then the other prevailed. Change. Resist. Change. Resist. By fits and starts of each, another New South was born.

These then are the energy sources that helped define the South you will meet in this collection of essays. Produced by

3

some of the finest tellers of the Southern tale, they suggest the shape and the shaping of the South at the time of the Democratic National Convention of 1988. The event is important for, taken in conjunction with the decision of the Republicans to convene in New Orleans, it suggests that the reunion may indeed be finally at hand.

Two of these writers are native to other regions and bring gifts of discovery and scholarship. David Halberstam witnessed the last great struggle between resistance and change, the civil rights movement, with the detachment of an outside observer, while Elizabeth Fox-Genovese dispassionately examines the historical record for a stark portrait of the daily life that lies behind the myth of the Old South.

Each of the others illuminates, however briefly, a characteristic of the region. Taken together, these pieces help suggest how and why it is as it is. You will find here the longing to hold and touch and perpetuate the family past. You will find a statement of possibilities lost by those who chose exile over servitude. Just so, you will find a testament to the strength of those who have returned to renew ancient claims. Again and again, you will find resistance and change. Portraits of women, black and white, are painted in new hues. The imprint left by the shape of the land is examined. The recent exit of the strutting demagogue is mourned, the political power of the church wondered at, the redneck finds a champion. And, from an exquisite essay on mothers and sons, you will understand why the region's sense of itself prevails.

Taken together, they paint in broad, often disconnected strokes the sense of this place at this time. Much is left unsaid, but the moment offered by these historic political conventions has given us an opportunity to stop and take a measure of what we have become. Perhaps there rests here, too, a hint of where we may be bound.

Bill Kovach
Editor
The Atlanta Journal-Constitution

Preface

Alex Haley

It was at the family home in Henning, Tennessee, where Alex Haley first heard the stories that inspired him to write the international best seller, Roots. *Haley is still crafting literature, which he hopes will be his greatest monument. The author, who won a special Pulitzer Prize for the book tracing his roots back through slavery to Africa, first won fame as co-creator of* The Autobiography of Malcolm X *after spending twenty years in the U.S. Coast Guard. He is completing* Henning, *a non-fiction book about his hometown in the west Tennessee flatlands, and two of three more books in progress have Tennessee settings. One focuses on a fictional Appalachian family. The other is a state history. With Sarah (Minnie Pearl) Cannon, Haley served as honorary chair of the successful Tennessee Homecoming, which brought former residents back for visits in 1986, and he says he has never lost his love for the South, despite the region's history of slavery, segregation and racial discrimination. "There's more substance here, so much more to write about," he has said. "I don't know anything I treasure more as a writer than being a Southerner. I love to write about the South and try to convey the experience of it ... the history of it. It has been pointed at negatively in so many ways, and so few people for a long time appreciated the physical beauty of the South."* ∎

Out of the Past, Into the Convention

*I*n my boyhood in the twenties in Henning, Tennessee (population four hundred seventy-five), my maternal grandfather, proud owner and operator of the W.E. Palmer Lumber Company, occupied something close to the status of a living legend among the blacks who made up roughly half the town's population. Even the whites gave Grandpa real respect, especially politically.

At no other time was this quite so evident as on Saturday afternoons late in the summer preceding a presidential election. At an early hour on those afternoons, yet another group of local black male personages invited by Grandpa would arrive at our home, each of them clad in his Sunday best. They were a mix of Methodists and Baptists (our family being the former). Some were landowning farmers, though most farmers were renters. There were ministers, both regular and itinerant, plus other church officers and elders. There were building craftsmen, teachers, undertakers, handymen and men of whatever other respectable positions were available in our county of Lauderdale in west Tennessee.

Somberly seated in the living room and the adjoining library and music room in Grandpa's residence (a house of unprecedented size and substance for a black family in Henning, it is today a Tennessee state museum), all of the men nodded and smiled stiffly. And at the appropriate moment, they held out their calloused and knob-knuckled hands to receive from my matriarchal grandma, my schoolteacher mama and a representative couple of church sisters the light repast of deftly served lemonade and finger sandwich choices of either salmon or chicken salad.

For the next ninety minutes or so, the assembled men would engage in an intense discussion of how the National Republican Party might be moved this year to better address the needs of local black people. It was a futile exercise. The men assembled in that room stood about as close to the Oval Office of a Republican White House as they did to the planet Mars. It was de facto knowledge that the lily-white state Republican Party held utterly no concern for any black interests and clearly did not even want any black colleagues. But Henning's black Republicans, though marooned within a sea of Democrats in the South, still proudly and persistently carried the tattered banner of their revered Grand Old Party of Lincoln, the Great Emancipator, even though they were not only powerless, but also racially ostracized by that party, as were the blacks of a thousand similar little agrarian townships.

My father later told me that many of the men who met in our home were members of a historic black confederation in the South known as "The Lincoln League." Its messiah was Mr. Robert Church Jr. (1885 -1952), who was thought to be "the richest colored man within the U.S. South," my dad said, and who was without question the most politically powerful black man in the United States at the time.

Remembering boyhood experiences plus the things Dad had told me, as we filmed *Roots: The Second Generation,* more than half a century later, I included a scene of how my grandpa, after hosting his own round of political meetings, journeyed with Dad, a young professor, to Memphis, where they were among some similarly select gatherings of black leaders invited by Mr. Church Jr. to his mansion.

At this elevated level of black Republican politics, the issues urgently discussed were such questions as what philanthropic monies — Rosenwald, Phelp-Stokes, Carnegie or other — were available for black community schools, libraries,

When not writing in the isolation of his cabin on some freighter at sea, the author frequently gathers friends from across the country at his one-hundred-fifty-year-old farm north of Knoxville.

YMCAs or YWCAs or parks. They talked of which cities and towns had priority with those funds, and how further political patronage could be obtained from the National Republican Party and whether visible jobs such as those held by the handful of blacks working already as federal mail clerks and carriers could be expanded in number.

At those meetings, visiting church officials would sometimes pointedly and proudly deposit surplus church funds with the Mr. Church Jr. banking interests. Some other visitors sought the advice of master politician Church on real estate matters. His late father, Mr. Robert Church Sr., had holdings in real estate that were among the largest in Memphis. In fact, during early Reconstruction, Mr. Church Sr. was one of a handful of wealthy men — the wealthiest in Memphis — who personally bought enough municipal bonds to help the nearly bankrupt city regain its charter.

Republican Church Jr. maintained his power even though Memphis was solidly within the Southern Democratic Party structure, autocratically controlled in Memphis by "Boss" Crump. Because it posed no threat to him, Crump, one of the most powerful machine politicians in the country, chose to let the fiefdom of the local black Republican coexist.

Back in our hometown of Henning that November, when the national elections were held, the voting was done by slips of paper that were marked, folded and then dropped into boxes placed in Raines' Feed Store, which was also where our town's trials were held. Henning's black Republicans always were the first voters to arrive on election morning, perhaps a maximum of fifty men, and always one woman, good Baptist sister Scrap Green, who year after year defied all opposition to the exercise of her right to vote. But Sister Scrap, just like the black men, voted quietly and was quickly gone. None of them elected to be around when, later in the day, some whites arrived with their spirits raised by Prohibition whiskey.

It is poignant how little attention history has paid to the

fact that from the early years of Reconstruction, in many Southern localities, the Republican Party's principal custodians were these and similar groups of blacks who voted in each national election as an act of holy ritual, no matter what obstacles were thrust into their paths, including physical threats. And there is irony in the fact that the blacks felt themselves so bonded to the Republican Party of Lincoln — because that helped keep alive the reason the Republican Party tended to be so despised among most whites of the defeated South.

And then, in 1932, a black population impoverished by the century's greatest depression was swept from their traditional political loyalties by the arrival over the airwaves of the charismatic Franklin Delano Roosevelt and his New Deal.

What he had promised when campaigning, he soon backed up after being elected — with his unprecedented, creative programs. None of it was distant or abstract — it was all practical, and personal, reaching literally into lives, into pocketbooks, into the very fields where longtime traditional black Republicans had picked and plowed.

The alphabetical array of NRA, WPA, CCC and FHA represented not only new governmental presences but also new hopes. Indeed, a new spirit *was* abroad in the land. For the first time, the first time *ever*, really, the black masses were being dealt with more as human beings, as Americans with the same needs and rights as white people.

One does well to remember the past. It gives a better perspective on some of the things that are happening in the present. It makes me think, for instance, that symbolically, in America today, there could hardly have been a better place than Atlanta for the Democratic National Convention.

Consider that not all that many rains ago, as the homeland Africans say, Atlanta was just one more medium-size, historic city in the South. Today, its commerce and influence stretch to the four corners of the Earth, returning business to enrich the region of the South and the nation of the United States.

It seems somehow fateful — and it seems a wonderful omen — that the city which a century and a quarter ago symbolized the devastation of the South has risen so far, and that it has done it in the last decade and a half under the successive administrations of two black mayors, first Maynard Jackson and now Andrew Young, both of whom, as a fellow Southerner, I'm so proud to call my friends. ∎

I.

The Southern Difference

C. Vann Woodward

*He has been called by his biographer John Herbert Roper "the dominant force in Southern historiography and one of the major forces in American historiography." And as evidenced in book after book, C. Vann Woodward has devoted his life to defining a region that seems well on its way to becoming a vital partner in shaping the American future. Nowhere is that prospect better symbolized than in the decision of both Democrats and Republicans to head south for their 1988 national conventions. Who better can place the region's contemporary rise in the context of its past power and glory — and ignominy, too — than Woodward himself? Born in Vanndale, Arkansas, the acclaimed professor of history emeritus at Yale University earned his undergraduate degree at Atlanta's Emory University, a master's at Columbia and his doctorate at the University of North Carolina at Chapel Hill. Wood-*ward's reputation has soared since his influential Origins of the New South *won the Bancroft Prize in 1951. His 1960 collection of essays,* The Burden of Southern History, *suggested that the South's experience both with the evils of slavery and with losing a war not only might have permanently stigmatized the region but also made it uniquely equipped to contribute to the development of a more humane national future. In 1982, he won the Pulitzer Prize in history for* Mary Chesnut's Civil War. ∎

The Particular Politics
Of Being Southern

*I*t has been a long time since the South has enjoyed the feeling of being really wanted and needed in the national business of electing a president. But now rather suddenly, and for the first time in history, both major political parties have held their presidential nominating conventions in the Deep South. Their choice could hardly have been dictated by the appeal of the region's climate — not in midsummer. No, it had to do with political considerations, with the perception that Southern votes would have a special importance in determining the outcome of the 1988 presidential election.

The resulting sense in the South is that of being once more a vital part of things, of being wanted and sought out after so long a time. It brings back images of power and glory long past. But even more powerfully, it recalls memories of isolation and relative impotence during the last century.

For almost fifty of the seventy-two years from Washington to Lincoln, Southern men held the presidency and a comparable share of other major offices. But in the next century, from Andrew Johnson through Lyndon Johnson, only one Southerner, a non-resident named Woodrow Wilson, was elected president, and no other achieved so much as the nomination of a major party for that office. Between Franklin Pierce in 1852 and Franklin Roosevelt in 1932, no winning candidate based his victory on popular majorities in both North and South, as most of them had in the past.

18

The South's long political isolation paralleled the lean years of the Democratic Party. In those years, between James Buchanan and FDR, the party elected only two presidents. Although Democrats relied much on the South for those victories, what political influence the South had in the lean years derived mainly from being a majority in a minority party. Another source of influence lay in the choice of Democratic presidential candidates. In those days, the old two-thirds rule dictated the proportion of convention ballots for nomination — a means Southern politicians found useful in discouraging undesirable candidates.

The need for the South's support and influence in presidential politics declined even more after 1932. Franklin Roosevelt could have lost every Southern state each time and still won all four of the elections from 1932 through 1944. So could Harry Truman in 1948 and Lyndon Johnson in 1964. Only Jack Kennedy and Jimmy Carter, each a rather special case, had to carry some Southern states in order to win. But six of the eight Democratic presidential election victories since 1932 were brought off by majorities that made Southern support unnecessary. And in 1936, the old two-thirds rule for nomination went by the board.

The change from power and influence to isolation and impotence was by no means an unfamiliar experience in the South. Change, in fact, has long been a central theme of Southern history, prodigious change of such degree and frequency as to become one of the region's several distinctive traits. Two great eras of change that were especially disjunctive stand out: The first came in two phases following the Civil War, the other in recent decades following World War II. More than any others, the changes after the Civil War were massive, sudden and traumatic for whites and blacks. They combined simultaneous changes in basic human relations that sometimes take centuries to occur but here took place in short order. They were forcibly imposed changes in relations between master and slave, classes and races, citizens and state, men and land — all collectively labeled Reconstruction.

Hard on all that followed the New South, a buzzing confusion of changes, some of which merely turned Reconstruction upside down in the name of reconciliation between estranged races, classes and sections. In charge of the New South confusion was a new class of businessmen, politicians and editors who promised salvation through Yankee-style enterprise and industrialization. They also swore that their program was miraculously consistent with the ideals, values and traditions of the Old South. Indeed, the Lost Cause had a hallowed place in the New South gospel. Consistent or not, and whether as planned or promised, changes did come in a flood tide that reached a crest in the last decade of the century. Incongruities and contradictions tumbled over one another madly.

Radicalism and reaction intermingled in the nineties. There were Populism and racism, farmer rebellion and urban arrogance, religious fervor and a peak in lynching. No sooner had a boom started than a depression set in. Innovations came on too fast to understand or accept — Jim Crow and jazz and disfranchisement and Coca-Cola and white primaries and trolley cars. And for a time, in the multiplication of towns, stores, railroads, mines, factories and jobs, came some of the economic wonders promised by the New South prophets. This was change with a vengeance, more than a traditional society like the South seemed able to absorb.

Then change and progress and innovation tapered off and in many places came to a halt. A long period of stagnation, backwardness and oppression set in that lasted almost the first half of the century. It lasted so long that the impression grew that nothing much ever changed in the South. That idea was encouraged by the yearnings of the many Southerners for continuity and the traditional ways of the past. Change has regularly met with resistance, often stubborn and intransigent resistance. For some, the long stagnation, because of the very absence of change, came as a relief.

C. Vann Woodward

From the vantage point of his home office in New Haven, Connecticut, historian C. Vann Woodward wrote anew about the past and future of his native South, a region where political life has grown more diverse.

21

The people of the South paid dearly for this perception. Their per capita wealth was usually less than half the national average, their per capita income was forty percent lower, their wages in manufactures were shamefully lower than elsewhere and for the sixty percent who worked in extractive industries, the pay was even lower than that. For long years most of the South remained a tributary, agricultural and raw-material economy, much of it a colonial dependency subservient to Northern interests.

These circumstances naturally had an effect upon the style of politics practiced by those who defended the system. The art of politics in the South long consisted, to a large extent, of resisting change or of giving it the appearance of continuity, and of contriving innovations in the guise of tradition. Given the genius that enabled the advocates of the New South in the 1880s to present their handiwork as perfectly in harmony and continuity with the Old South, almost anything of the sort seemed possible. The art is reflected in the political personalities who practiced it, and it helps to account for the impression of paradox in the political scene and the frequent outcropping of antique gestures and quaint mannerisms among Southern statesmen.

In their plight as an isolated political minority, Southern leaders sought ways to protect themselves from the demands of majority will. David M. Potter, a gifted historian who came from Georgia, has shown how they found guidance and inspiration in the strategies of an antebellum statesman whose doctrines they had repudiated in theory but adopted in practice. This was the South Carolina Machiavelli, John C. Calhoun, who called his doctrine "the concurrent majority." It provided various veto or "negating" devices by which minorities could defend themselves against majorities, and long after Calhoun and the ill-starred cause on which he lavished his remarkable genius had passed away, his idea took on new life among his successors.

To congressmen from a minority region who constituted a majority of the Democratic minority in the House and Senate, Calhoun's schemes were highly useful. Thirty of the South's seats in the House came by virtue of a black population not permitted to vote, a number enhanced by a bonus of twelve because of the emancipation the South had failed to prevent. Under the old antebellum rule in which three-fifths of the slave population was counted toward the South's representation in Congress, eighteen House seats were produced. But with the Emancipation Proclamation and the passage of the Fourteenth Amendment, the black population was counted whole. It gave the South thirty seats, and the white political establishment controlled them and used them to one-party advantage. Between Reconstruction and the New Deal, the Southern wing of the Democratic Party in Congress was almost always larger than the Northern wing. This meant, among other things, a majority in party caucuses and some control over them in both houses.

In the sixty years of Southern ascendancy among Democratic congressmen, the neo-Calhounians perfected the system and elaborated its machinery with the filibuster and unlimited debate in the Senate; obstructionist brakes of the Rules Committee in the House; the two-thirds rule in Democratic nominating conventions; the autonomy of committee chairmen in Congress; and with the seniority system of congressional hierarchy. Those were the days of the Solid South, the one-party South with all its marbles in one bag. The old party was then as sacred as the Lost Cause, and, as Potter said, "God was in his heaven, and the traditional interests of the South were secure," not to mention the interests of the conservative rulers of the region and at least a minority of their white constituency.

For all the ingenuity of the Southern stratagems and devices and the skill with which they were manipulated, the system was essentially designed to prevent rather than to accomplish things. It was best at resisting rather than initiating change, at preventing the worst choice rather than achieving the most desirable one. It left more monuments of compromise than of legislation. Its statesmen were more eloquent about the lessons of the past than the possibilities of the future. Their negative and cautionary approach did not pull them to the front and center when national decisions of change and innovation were at stake. They grew accustomed in those circumstances to taking a back seat and being resigned to an offstage presence.

After 1932, the South elected fewer than half the Democratic members of Congress and suffered a historical transition from constituting a majority wing in a minority party to constituting a minority wing of a majority party. This undermined the old system and put the South on notice that its tenure on negative power had a limited future. Nevertheless, the traditional mechanism did not fall apart immediately. Such devices as the filibuster, the seniority system, the powerful committee chairmen and the caucus had taken deep roots and were defended in stubborn rear-guard actions. In spite of defeats, the running battle continued for thirty years and more.

The rule of seniority proved the most durable of the devices, and for the South it had a special importance. No other party in the country produced congressmen who could rival the seniority rolled up regularly by Southern delegations in Washington. With no opposition party to face after the Populists were put down and only white primaries to contend with in those days, most Southern Democrats enjoyed a smoothly paved road to seniority. A lion's share of power followed from a lion's share of seniority. In 1893, the South held thirty-six of the forty-four most senior Democratic seats in the House of Representatives, and twenty years later, it had all but five of the fifty-eight most senior seats.

The increments of seniority lingered on. In 1931 the two senior members of the Senate were both from North Carolina. As time passed, Harry Byrd of Virginia, "Cotton Ed" Smith of South Carolina, Kenneth McKellar of Tennessee, Richard Russell of Georgia, Lister Hill of Alabama, Allen Ellender of Louisiana, Walter George of Georgia and Carter

Glass of Virginia all served more than thirty years in the Senate. These records were far outstripped in the House, where in 1961, Sam Rayburn of Texas and Carl Vinson of Georgia were serving their twenty-fifth terms — almost a half-century each of consecutive service.

Such venerable figures were the very stuff of legend, and with their blend of rustic urbanity, they loved to live up to the role. A folksy lot of Machiavellis they were, but no less the masters of power. It was power as real as it comes in a democracy, and for all the casualness and informality with which it was wielded, it was quite palpable, quite tangible. If some of those who wielded it could be loved and admired, they could also be envied and feared. Everybody knew "Mr. Sam," but much depended on how well and on what terms. When young Lyndon Johnson sat at the feet of old Sam Rayburn, the power lines of authority popped and crackled with the high voltage being transmitted. The old system was still working in the thirties.

Then in the forties and on through the sixties came another great storm of social change and economic upheaval with more shocks than the South had sustained since the 1860s, and perhaps as many as it suffered then. Old monuments and institutions were overturned or swept away completely. One-party politics went the way of one-crop agriculture and the one-horse farmer, and gone with them and the wind were the poll tax, the white primary, the Jim Crow laws and the white man's monopoly on the ballot box. In their place came civil rights, the Brown decision, integrated schools, biracial voting and bipartisan politics. Cattle replaced cotton, blacks moved north, Yankees moved south and everybody moved to town.

The storm of social change took its toll on the old political system and the devices of control that the Southern bloc had used so long and effectively. In 1948, four Southern states bolted the Democratic Party for the Dixiecrats, and there has been no Solid South since. In 1964, Barry Goldwater won only in states that hadn't voted Republican since

Reconstruction, Southern states, and lost in every state that had ever so voted. There is no longer any majority party in the South. The Democrats are simply one of two minority parties. This as compared with 1952, when, by self-identification, Democrats outnumbered Republicans nearly eight to one, and among native whites ten to one.

By 1984, party identifications among whites were thirty-three percent Democrats and twenty-nine percent Republicans, with blacks overwhelmingly Democratic. The Democratic defectors mainly became independents. Conservatives prevail among remaining Southern Democrats, accounting for fifty-six percent as compared with twenty-seven percent liberal or leaning that way. Taking the leanings of independents into account, however, Democrats still retain a slight advantage over Republicans. It is clear that conservative Democrats now have to mind their minority Ps and Qs for the need of black votes to eke out a majority. In presidential elections, there appear to be alluring prospects below the Potomac for Republicans.

The South of today is undoubtedly more like the rest of the country than ever before in many ways, politics included. That is not to say, however, that it has lost its distinctiveness or become homogenized USA. The power of the old Southern bloc in Congress, now divided between parties, is only a shadow of what it once was. In 1964, for the first time in history, a Democratic Senate imposed cloture of debate on its Southern members. Their power in the Rules Committee has been curtailed, and it has been curbed in other ways as well. As a vehicle of entrenched power for the South, for states rights and white supremacy, the Democratic Party no longer exists.

If the song has ended, however, the melody lingers on. It lingers in the number of powerful committees of Congress with Southern chairmen by virtue of their seniority. It lingers in flashes of political genius and the skills of surviving masters, talents desperately needed in crises of 1988. It lingers as well in occasional throwbacks to Populist rhetoric, in outcroppings of old-fashioned oratory and in gestures of quaint courtesy just to assure constituents that, if nothing else, traditions are still respected and all is not lost in change and flux. It is a regional, not a racial heritage, and black politicians long ago mastered it and are now more free to practice it. The blend of old and new political cultures staves off homogenization and helps to preserve a jealously cherished distinctiveness.

The remaining distinctiveness, however, no longer comes at the cost of isolation, withdrawal or intransigence on the part of the South, or rejection and indifference on the part of the rest of the country, as it once did. The South no longer looks to the past for its guidelines, and it faces a future of opportunity and national influence — the promise of once more being wanted and needed. One significant evidence of that promise comes from the two major party conventions held this year in the lower South. Surely they were the more welcome for that reason. ∎

David Halberstam

Fresh from Harvard, New York-born David Halberstam came South in 1955 with a sense of intellectual and emotional mission, and found himself at the beginning of an era. Intensely interested in moral and ethical questions, the son of Jewish immigrants from Poland had read Swedish sociologist Gunnar Myrdal's An American Dilemma: The Negro Problem and Modern Democracy, *and he wanted to see for himself how the South was dealing with race. Three decades later, he is one of the nation's most respected journalists and the author of ten books, including the monumental trilogy on power,* The Best and the Brightest, The Powers That Be *and* The Reckoning. *Future books will focus on the social-cultural history of the fifties and the baseball pennant race of 1949. Now living in New York City and on Nantucket Island, Halberstam worked as a stringer for the* Boston Globe *in college but began his full-time professional career as a reporter for the West Point [Mississippi]* Daily Times Leader *before moving to the* Nashville Tennessean. *Reporting for* The New York Times *from 1960 to 1967, he became controversial for his penchant for questioning the official version of events in Vietnam. Though his reporting infuriated two presidents, including Lyndon Johnson, who called him "a traitor to his country," Halberstam won a Pulitzer Prize for international reporting in 1964.* ∎

In the Eye of the Storm: The South in 1955

I went south in June of 1955, in search of drama, I suppose, as much as anything. That is my judgment now, though thirty-three years ago, my motivation was probably more complicated. There is drama all around us, of course: A good short-story writer knows that there is drama in the loss of a child's favorite stuffed animal, and our best playwrights, Williams and Miller, have taught us that one need not venture from the home in search of compelling drama. But journalists, particularly twenty-one-year-old beginners as I was, are more primitive in their knowledge of what constitutes drama. They are at their best instant witnesses, but witnesses of the exterior not the interior. Thus then did the South beckon.

The year I graduated from college, I sensed that something important was about to happen, and it was not going to happen in the great cities of the North. I wanted to be a witness. So upon graduation, I set out for Mississippi in my 1946 Chevrolet with a record player, a few books (chiefly *An American Dilemma*, by Gunnar Myrdal, sworn enemy of all those many segregationists who had never read him) secreted away in the back of the car, and all my hopes. I knew nothing about race in America.

Two years earlier, as an aspiring nineteen-year-old reporter on the *Harvard Crimson*, I had been working at the paper almost alone one night. That day, Dwight Eisenhower had announced that he was nominating Earl Warren to be

30

the chief justice of the United States. The court was then still considering Brown v. Board of Education. Earl Warren, a former governor of California and the Republican vice presidential nominee in 1948, had played an important role in tilting the 1952 convention from Taft to Eisenhower.

I called and interviewed the most knowledgeable professors at Harvard Law School for their reactions. To a man, they were critical of so *political* an appointment. The court, they agreed, should be above petty politics of this sort. They kept referring to something called "the Warren Court," the first time I had ever heard that phrase, and they suggested that it might be a disaster for civil rights. I dutifully reported their negative reactions. And so with this vast experience in civil rights, this great fund of knowledge, I set off for the South to cover the coming revolution.

June 1955 was a moment of relative calm: A little more than a year after the law of the land had been changed, it was still several years before the broad social, political and legal assault upon the almost monolithic fabric of segregation would take place, an assault that in the end was nothing less than a revolution.

Brown v. Board of Education had signaled with utter finality the end of legal segregation, although a series of ancillary decisions was still to come, and it had irrevocably thrown the force of the federal government behind integration. But nothing had happened yet.

It was also a nervous time, a time of rumor feeding fear feeding rumor feeding fear. The South was still as it had been, segregated, readying itself to resist. Some politicians were already rushing in to enhance their careers by promising that they would be the leaders of the new instant resistance. They were eager to make promises that could not be kept.

A generation of Southern politicians who should have known better told their people that there was a peaceful way to face down the Supreme Court through a doctrine, almost incomprehensible to anyone who tried to understand it, called Interposition. As I write this word, one that I have not typed in almost thirty years, it seems more implausible than ever, the promise of charlatans. The attractive thing about it, I suppose, was the idea that it *sounded* constitutional.

With Interposition, no one would have to go to jail for resisting the government in Washington, and no one would be hurt. That was good, because it was important for the governing establishments, state by state, town by town, to feel good about themselves. White people comforted themselves that the black people in their communities did not want integration (better schools, better jobs, better housing, fairer treatment by the courts and police). They were perfectly content with the status quo. There was wide agreement upon this.

The source for this wisdom inevitably turned out to be someone's maid. Rarely in American history have so many domestic employees been so religiously quoted by their employers. All maids were against the NACCP, as it was known. All maids thought that the folks down in the South would be all right if the folks up in the North would just leave them alone. A joke soon went around about two maids talking together. The first maid told the second that she had been at the fanciest party given in the town in years. A roast beef dinner with a choice of two desserts. "Who was there?" asked the second.

"The mayor and his wife, the sheriff and his wife, the president of the bank and his wife, the president of the factory and his wife and the district attorney and his wife," said the first.

"You're certainly right about it being fancy," said the second, "but what were those high-class white folks talking about?"

"Us," answered the first.

I spent that year working on a small daily in northeast Mississippi. I had come to Mississippi seeking drama, and I found it there every day: Decisions and relationships that in a Northern city would surely have been boring and mundane were not so for me here. There because everything was touched by race, I was never bored.

It was there I found for the first time in my life the value of a book. Not the pleasure — I had always known the pleasure — but the value. The book in question was the Myrdal, a true epic. By all rights, sociological treatise that it was, it should have been dry and heavy. Instead, it was wonderfully well-written and infinitely alive. I worked, after all, that year, without senior colleagues to talk to and compare notes with every day. And so, I turned at the end of the day to Myrdal, and that which I needed was always there; that which I had seen he had seen, and could confirm; that which puzzled me, he could explain. Never before and never since has a book meant so much to me: friend, teacher, confidant. It was unfailingly accurate and sensitive. It was as if someone had written a book about the town I was in, only a few years before I got there. Because of him, I was never alone.

I found everywhere the conflict between the world as it was and the world as it was perceived to be: segregation was oppressive, but those who did the oppressing quite naturally did not like to feel like oppressors, and so they had created an elaborate rationale that would give the appearance of the consent of the oppressed.

Few understood that what the blacks felt was revealed not so much in what they said but in what they didn't say, in those long silences, or in the irony of their humor. Acquiescence was by no means acceptance. The quickness with which an ordinary black — if he decided that he was free to speak his mind — switched from the head-nodding Tom of everyday manner to a rather proud antagonist was sometimes startling.

Once that year while I was working on a piece for *The Reporter* then a liberal magazine, I spent some time on a plantation in Sunflower County in the Delta. I found myself with a handful of blacks in one of the county's tiny villages. These were true sharecroppers. Somehow they decided on their own that I was a federal agent — nothing I could say would convince them that I was a merely a reporter. I suppose it was the look — Ivy League clothes, tie, glasses, Eastern accent. The more I protested, the more they were convinced that I was a secret agent of some sort. I was stunned by their outpouring of resentment toward their station, stunned not by what they felt, but the openness with which they, people of complete vulnerability, expressed it.

The old order still held in 1955. That which had been still was. Rural Mississippi was a lot like the rural part of any Deep South state, divided by class, divided by race, embattled, impoverished and largely bypassed by the Industrial Revolution, which in the middle of the twentieth century was bestowing such remarkable affluence on the rest of the nation. The South, I think, with less economic opportunity than the rest of the country, was less meritocratic in those heady days after World War II.

It held on to a social fabric that was changing rapidly elsewhere. Therefore, divisions about class mattered. The maiden names of young women in a town's upper class were important because they still held important clues to the town's pecking order. I suspect that Harvard in the mid-fifties, though it was known as an old boy school, probably had a far higher percentage of students whose parents had not been to college than Ole Miss did.

In towns such as West Point, where I worked, there was little in the way of new money, and for that matter, little in the way of old money either. Class and race mattered because often they were all a person had. A white man who made four thousand dollars a year had a good job, and he had a right to wear a shirt and tie and jacket, and that was important.

Industrial jobs were hard to come by: That year, I wrote an endless series of stories about the one new factory starting up in town, a place where the owner was going to re-tin large milk cans. Getting this factory was felt to be a considerable coup for West Point. The owner employed I think,

Central Park, near the Halberstam apartment, provides the author respite while he is working on two book projects.

fewer than five workers. Then I saw it as a story; now I see it as a sign of the limits of possibilities in that small town.

Segregation was absolute, and blacks were utterly power-less and disorganized, with no active political leadership. (That new leadership would surge forth in just a few years with the Montgomery bus boycott and the rise of a new gen-eration of well-educated black Christian ministers.)

Signs over public facilities, the most hated symbols of the system, still said "White Only." All of the state's schools were segregated. Any black who tried to argue that the law had changed, that the government in Washington had prom-ised change with all deliberate speed, became a target. If he signed a petition calling for the integration of a local school, he immediately lost his job. If he persisted longer, more dire fates awaited him.

I worked in Clay County, and when it came time for the Democratic primary, which in these days was the only elec-tion, Tom Tubb, who was our leading local politician, spoke at a public meeting and warned his electors not to let any of "them" vote. He used the N-word. If they showed up, he said, take them out in back and take care of them — and if you don't know how to do it, I'll teach you.

When I put that in my story, Henry Harris, my editor, tried to take it out. I insisted it stay in, that it had been said by one of the town's leading officials at a public meeting. We argued. "Well," said Henry in frustration, "can't you at least put in that Mr. Tubb was only trying to help them?" Missis-sippi was the hardest of the hardline states. A moderate Mississippi public official — and there were not that many moderates — was someone who did not like to talk about race, who did not seem to relish talking about the idea of how, by God, if this keeps up, if they don't realize their place, what we were going to do to them.

A moderate seemed embarrassed by all the hate that was stirring. A moderate said (in a moment of great privacy and trust) something like this: Well, yes, change was going to come, but it was going to be slow, damn slow, you can take my word for that, because I *know* these people, I grew up with them, both races, been with them all my life, and it damn well wouldn't happen in this century. A moderate used the word "nigra" instead of "nigger." A moderate tried to find the center ground. Mississippi was not fertile ground for moderates.

This was a rare moment in post-war America, a moment in which, in one state, there was no real freedom of speech. Mississippi — as Jim Silver, a liberal professor at Ole Miss (actually *the* liberal professor, as the whole state knew), aptly titled his book a few years later — Mississippi was a closed society. The entire governmental process, most of the religious establishment, most of the educational process and almost all of the journalistic process either endorsed segregation enthusiastically or paid lip service to it.

Those who offended, who spoke their minds, were systematically isolated — politically, economically or, perhaps worst of all in a small town, socially. For some native Mississippians, it was too much: They could remain on native soil, albeit with a fragmented conscience, untrue to what they had come to believe, or they could reluctantly leave.

A surprising number of the state's most interesting young people left. A few years later, living in New York for the first time in my adult life, I started hanging around with Willie Morris, recently of Yazoo City. He connected me to the vast subculture of Mississippians living in New York. I quickly picked up that when they talked, they spoke feverishly, not of events in New York or Vietnam, but of Mississippi. It was as if they were still there. Mississippi, I realized, was possibly the only state in the Union with its own set of people living in exile.

It was changing, of course, changing faster than anyone knew, although probably at that precise moment the change was mostly in perception. But it was coming. Some fifteen years later, writing a book about how we went to war in Vietnam, I found a phrase from Emerson in one of George Ball's dove papers that seemed perfect for what was happening in Mississippi in 1955: Events are in the saddle, Emerson wrote, and ride mankind. For Mississippi was not an island. It was attached to the whole.

I was young then and did not understand the word *agenda* as it is applied to national political focus, and I did not understand the fact that part of what shaped an agenda was national journalistic focus. Nor did I or many others in a pre-media society realize that the media spotlight was now as important as the political one: that in modern America — and this was the first example — the two were fatefully intertwined.

The political part of the agenda was easy enough to understand: Ten years had passed since the end of World War II, a war that had been an immensely egalitarian experience and that had helped to turn the nation back towards its egalitarian obligations. Certainly the court decisions being rendered had been simmering for a long time. Those decisions were conferring on the black cause a condition of legal legitimacy that would soon spread into moral legitimacy, as preached in both white and black churches and manifested in a new kind of non-violent activism.

But the media aspect was more supple. I could, being young and inexperienced, sense it but not define it. I knew viscerally that something was happening, that the nation was beginning to watch, and watch carefully. Possibly in some obscure part of my brain, that was one of the reasons I had gone South in the first place, on the assumption that people would be watching, and that if I performed well, they would be watching me.

That year the first great media event of what was to be the civil rights movement took place in Mississippi. It took place over in the Delta, in Tallahatchie County. Roy Bryant and J.W. Milam, referred to by everyone who knew them as rednecks, were accused of murdering a young black child from Chicago named Emmett Till because he had whistled at Bryant's wife.

The national media poured into the town of Sumner, as it had not appeared in a Southern small town in recent history. It was a momentous case. I decided to write a piece for *The Reporter* about the media's presence and role. I carefully subscribed to all the major Northern papers that covered the trial. I intended to make sense out of it all, find meaning, prove something, although what I did not know.

On my day off, I regularly drove over to Sumner and hung around with those giants of the Northern press. They were gods to me, for I wanted to be one of them. If a young man can fall in love with an older man because of that man's craft, then I had fallen in love with Murray Kempton of the *New York Post* because of what he was writing, columns that seemed to me almost perfect short stories.

My Sunday visits I would watch him from afar, moving elegantly among the others; I watched the respect he was given by his peers. DiMaggio walking through the Yankee clubhouse must have been accorded the same treatment, I thought. I did not dare to introduce myself.

We met seven years later at an awards ceremony and had a marvelous evening arguing over who was a greater international symbol of American culture. I said Ray Charles. He said Thelonious Monk. I still wonder which one of us was right.

I also remember in Sumner my first contact with the gallows humor of first-rate journalists. It is the kind of humor that could appreciate the sheriff of Tallahatchie County, an immense man named H.C. Strider. He seemed the perfect symbol of his county; he was a large landowner (he listed himself in the town's Yellow Pages under "plantation"), and he had painted the letters of his name on top of the huts where his sharecroppers lived. S-T-R-I-D-E-R. He was not in the best of moods about this trial and about the presence of the white reporters, come here to do Mississippi ill, and he seemed even angrier about having to deal with the few black reporters in a courtroom he by all rights considered his own.

His bad humor showed. Eventually he was told by his peers in the town establishment to display better manners to the visitors and to be more courteous to the black reporters. So each day, he dutifully went up to them and said, "Morning, niggers."

I did not pull off the piece I had in mind — I'm not sure in the end I even tried. My magazine skills were more limited then, and I did not have the conceptual tools to deal with something I sensed rather than understood. The piece eluded me. But I understand now what was happening. In that post-war era, there was as there had never been before a national press corps, and it had, because of the increased muscle of broadcast news, greater resonance and power than ever before, particularly with the coming of embryonic new evening television news shows.

To these men and the men who had assigned them, it was not the verdict, the eventual acquittal of Bryant and Milam that mattered; what mattered was the process, and that they as journalists were beginning to put Mississippi and the Southern system on trial. How segregation was maintained was now being scrutinized for the first time in what was to be a great nationally televised morality play.

I think the civil rights movement as we know it, an ongoing moral drama that forced ordinary people to come to terms with their consciences, began with the Till trial as much as it did with Brown v. Board of Education. The people of West Point did not like what was happening in Sumner. They were quite irate about it all: They were not killers, they protested, but then, of course, they were also unwilling to say publicly that what had happened was wrong and that it was a result of a system that offered complete judicial immunity to whites, no matter how loathsome, and none to blacks, no matter how honorable. The national press corps, they said angrily, was making it all seem black and white. And of course it was.

I left Mississippi in the middle of 1956. Technically, there had been no change. The schools were all white, segregation in all walks of life was still a fact of life. The White Citizens Councils were more powerful than ever. No one dared speak for integration.

But Mississippi was changing, even if there were few public signs of it. For something else was happening at that moment. Again, I did not realize it at the time. I said that Mississippi was connected to the whole. That was true not just legally and politically (the story is told of the Louisiana segregationist leader Leander Perez, who wanted nothing less than total resistance to integration. "Can't do it any-more, Leander," Governor Earl Long told him, "the feds have got the Bomb."). Even the Deep South was connected electronically to the whole.

In those years, for the first time, there was the beginning of a national television hookup that brought Mississippi into the nation. When Jackie Robinson and Roy Campanella and Willie Mays played baseball during a World Series, they did not merely play in Ebbetts Field or the Polo Grounds, they played in the homes of the white people of Mississippi as well.

I remember watching the World Series of 1955 with a cross section of Mississippians. They were all rooting for the Yankees against the Dodgers, which must have been painful enough. But one knew that even this last resort, a surviving all-white team to root for, was an illusion; the clock was tick-ing. The talent of those first black players was almost lumi-nescent. Not to be impressed was not to love baseball. The only option, and these men knew and loved baseball, was to turn off the television set and walk out on the World Series.

In the past, segregation meant denial for blacks: Now for the first time, it might mean denial for whites instead. (A few years later, in 1960, I was covering Lyndon Johnson's campaign for vice president. It was at the height of the crisis over integrating the University of Georgia. A reporter friend from *The New York Times* told me that he was worried that the Georgia authorities might close the university. I assured him that that would never happen. "Why not?" he asked, somewhat puzzled by my confidence. "Because that would mean giving up University of Georgia football and not playing in the SEC, and the people of this state will not do it. Football is what binds this state together," I answered. Some twenty-two years later, I drove across the same state and saw bumper stickers that proclaimed, "Herschel Walker Is My Cousin.")

T he price of bigotry was clearly going up. It was no longer the country that was different, it was Mississippi that was different, Mississippi that would have to change. The early television entertainment shows such as *Ed Sullivan* used a large number of black entertainers. That, too, was a source of daily anger among those in the local power structure. There was talk of boycotting the companies that sponsored *Sullivan*. (I remember considerable talk of boycotting Ford, though it always seemed to me that there were as many Fords on the road as ever.) But what was true was that it was happening, the country was changing, and Mississippians were going to watch — and be watched — as the procession continued.

I did not know all of that then. Sometimes things that I thought were important turned out to be less important, and things that I barely noticed as social indicators — Jackie Robinson stealing home, and the accompanying groan that was half pain and half admiration — turned out to be important. But it was happening, and happening quickly. In ten years, the groundwork — legal, social and now, finally, political — was laid. It had happened.

About the time that I was in Mississippi, a young man named Frank Clement ran for governor of Tennessee, promising that he would *never* integrate the state's schools. "Never . . . ," reflected his opponent, Gordon Browning. "never is a long time." A few years later, while I was a reporter in Nashville, Frank Clement used the state National Guard to help escort black children into integrated schools. One of the reasons for Clement's change of heart was his burning ambition for higher office. Never in Tennessee had lasted for about three years.

It was painful. And no less than in other parts of the country, race remains a difficult and painful subject. But people do change, and they do learn to live with each other. Four years ago, when Jesse Jackson campaigned for the presidency, he apologized at the end for any remarks that might have offended. That, he said, was "not my truest self." When he said it, I thought not so much of him but of the people I had known in the South, caught between vast social change and their own traditions. It was a hard time for ordinary people. Sometimes probably what showed was indeed their "truest" selves. Sometimes, less often, it was their better selves.

I am aware of the change every time I go back to the South now, of constant change, of a better, more vibrant, more optimistic society. This past year I watched the hearings on Supreme Court nominee Robert Bork, and I watched as votes from the Deep South defeated him.

I am not naive about the politics behind each vote, but I am aware as well that there must have been a feeling on the part of some of those Southern senators that not only did they not want to go through those violent and volatile years again — it had been done once and once was enough — but that whatever misgivings each senator had about the new social contract that exists today, there was a consensus that it is a better and more just region now than it was then, that for the first time the South was free of the worst of a terrible past. That for the first time it has a real chance at the future. ■

II.

Politics:
A Tradition in Change

Ferrol Sams Jr.

Living just down the road from Atlanta in Fayette-ville, where his family has nurtured the ground for generations and where he has practiced medicine since 1951, Dr. Ferrol Sams Jr. watches over his patients intently and casts an anecdotal eye about him to gather material for novels and short stories. Both of his novels, Run With the Horsemen *in 1982 and its sequel,* The Whisper of the River, *were regional best sellers, as was his 1987 collection of short stories,* The Widow's Mite. *He has completed a coffee-table book,* The Passing: Perspectives of Rural America, *in collaboration with artist Jim Harrison, and a third novel is in progress. "Where I come from," he has said, "your main problem is not that you're going to write and make up stories to tell. Your main problem is toning down those stories so that some innocent reader will believe them and say this is a great writer of fiction." The razor-witted physician has never allowed himself the luxury of intellectual distance. For twenty-four years, he served in local politics as a city council member. Recently he became embroiled in another controversy: the attempt by Fundamentalists to stem a supposedly liberal tide at Mercer University. A Mercer alumnus, Sams defends the university's academic freedom. Raised a Baptist, he backslid years ago when he married "a beautiful Philistine princess" and converted to her denomination: Methodism.* ■

God as Elector:
Religion and the Vote

sed to, a long time ago when I was just a lad of a boy, we made do with what we had. No roads were paved; my part of the country was laced with meandering trails that were, depending on the season, dust beds over washboard or quagmires of clutching mud. Travel was either an adventure or a nightmare. The roads were maintained by local chain gangs; political bosses did not have the option of procuring state funds for paving.

There was no electricity and consequently no refrigerators, washing machines, vacuum cleaners or televisions. I once said there was no running water, but one of my peers put the lie to me about that. She said that her family always had running water, especially in the wintertime. They ran out to the well to draw a bucketful and they ran back in the house with it.

There were no stockpiles of frozen foods in the grocery stores and, had there been, there was no money with which to purchase them. We raised what we ate, and what we did not raise we did without. Our choice of religion was just as restricted. One was either a Fundamentalist or one was a heathen. Period. Argumentative purists might assert that we had the option of being either Baptist or Methodist, since both denominations existed in the county. That is simply not true, for the religion into which one was born was where one stayed. Forever. To ultimate residence in Abraham's bosom. Voluntary change was unthinkable, and, when it occasionally occurred in the fervor of revival or the pique of personal affront, it branded one as wishy-washy and unstable, not steadfast in faith and, therefore, not to be trusted in other matters. Baptists outnumbered Methodists at least two to one, and Fundamentalism was one hundred percent.

In the heart of the post-Reconstruction, mid-Depression rural South, subjected to the most effective oppression these United States have ever practiced, mired to our buttocks in spine-stiffening poverty, we were not concerned in our churches with social change. We were concerned with salvation. We listened to quasi-literate zealots who supported themselves during the week at public work and preached in the hinterlands on alternate Sundays and the second week in August. They waved their arms, thumped their Bibles and roared the Gospel of the humble Jesus into our ears for one purpose only: that our immortal souls might be snatched from the searing flames of Eternal Hell. Any preacher who had ventured to voice an opinion on local politics would have been branded a meddlesome smart-aleck and driven from his pulpit for having dared to violate the doctrine of separation of Church and State. That premise had the authority of "render unto Caesar." The Bible was the cookbook of salvation, and the recipe had to be followed most carefully.

The taboo on politics was relaxed somewhat when Al Smith aspired to be president of the United States of America way up yonder in Washington, D.C. Preachers were forgiven brief but fervent references to that race; after all, the man was a Roman Catholic, tainted by the practice of idolatry, guilty of prostration before graven images in clear violation of scriptural admonitions against such behavior. Even had Catholicism not been condemned in the King James true and only disclosure of Divine Will, there was always one's grandmother to discourse in hushed tones upon the hopeless plight of the pupils of the Pope. Fundamentalism was as much a way of life as corn bread with turnip greens. So was being a Democrat. The choice, therefore, between a

Republican and a Roman Catholic was a divisive one; the furor it created could have been duplicated only had the candidates been devil and witch.

After four years of Hoover, local consensus was that we had chosen the former. The Reign of Roosevelt was met with rejoicing. Despite the head-wagging prophecy by some that we could not spend ourselves rich, there was gleeful acceptance of his economic reforms. The attitude of Georgia was encapsulated in the joke about a rural teacher leading her students through morning exercises.

"Children, who paved the road in front of your house?"

In response, the chorus, "Roosevelt!"

"Who put electricity into your house for you?"

"Roosevelt!"

"Who gave your uncle a job in the WPA?"

"Roosevelt!"

"Who got your granddaddy an old age pension?"

"Roosevelt!"

"All right, children. Now. Who made you?"

After a moment of silence one little boy asserted stoutly, "God."

Whereupon a gallused, barefoot towhead leaped up in the back row and yelled, "Throw that sorry Republican out of here."

Few Fundamentalists realized that there had now appeared a crack in the foundation of their faith. They were comparable to the Israelites who followed Moses through the perils of the wilderness only to be bedazzled at the moment of deliverance by the golden calf. Not one of us thought to compare Roosevelt to Aaron, yet under the hypnosis of that honeyed tongue, devout Christians offered up the protective jewelry of their principles. The sacred breastplate of the inerrancy of Scripture was flung into the fire of prosperity and was most effectively melted down. The day of the Calf of Gold was here, and we worshiped it. The very Baptists who scorned statues of the Virgin Mary now genuflected with alacrity. We even continued to call our country

Fayette County author Ferrol Sams visits the grounds of Woolsey Baptist Church where he worshiped before enrolling at Mercer University, a Baptist institution.

a democracy. The camel's head was in the tent, and its breath was sweet.

The rural South was led into the religious enlightenment of the twentieth century under a banner peppered with popular initials: RFD, NRA, CCC, WPA, TVA, NYA and others; but the most significant of them was FDR. We, of course, did not march in lock step or cadence, but we marched. A redoubtable girl one day proclaimed in class, "I don't care what you say about Columbus and Magellan; you ain't never going to make me believe the world is round because right there in my very own Bible, Jesus talks about angels holding up the four corners of the Earth." Everyone laughed. The teacher laughed, too. Our Protestant legacy of one hundred years of dedicated evangelism throughout the rural South had been advanced determinedly by zealous circuit riders. That legacy now gathered up its skirts and rode astride the horse of mirth, a steed fed and fattened on progress and prosperity.

My grandfather stands in my memory as a symbol of defiance. "By the sweat of thy brow shalt thou earn thy bread," he thundered. "I'll take no money I have not earned." When my father reasoned patiently with him that he had in reality earned an old age pension and then assured him that everyone else was doing it, he was silenced with a snort. "If I'd raised you children like that, not one of you would have amounted to a tinker's damn. I've taught all y'all that if you don't work, you don't eat. When I married your Ma in '75 I didn't even own any land, but I told her folks that if they set me down on a rock as flat as the pan of my hand, I'd manage to make a living for her. And by God, I have."

My grandmother daintily wiped a snuff stain from the corner of her mouth and confirmed, "We don't do things because everyone else does. We never have. Remember that you are in the world but not of this world." True Fundamentalism, the genuine article, died with my grandfather and is interred in the cemetery at Woolsey, Georgia.

Now our roads are paved. We have electricity, both blessing and bane to rural areas. Subdivisions are the main cash crop in our county now. More Yankees live among us than came through with Sherman, and it is against the law of the land today to shoot them. Fortunately, most of them did not bring matches this time. Progress is upon us, and, like it or not, we are in the twentieth century, an advent that may very well harelip Hell and half of Georgia.

I was raised in the middle-class South but taught that it was Upper Class. I have leaned in the past toward the attitude that ignorance is an absolute. Ignorance, I have now decided, is relative. We are surrounded, gradually but increasingly, by people who either cannot or do not read. An entire generation has been raised up that has never read the Bible or had it read to them. It is easier to plop a child down before a television screen than to hold him on one's lap and read the Storybook Bible aloud.

These are our Southern children; their ignorance is our doing. Their parents grew up reading the Bible themselves but became so enlightened that they snigger at snake handlers, shrug at Seventh-day Adventists, berate intrusive Jehovah's Witnesses, and patronizingly assert that Christian Scientists are neither Christian nor scientific.

I get the impression that we have abandoned the ideal of a Christian nation and that, indeed, in some circles in the South, it is all right if this is now a country of no religion whatever. I think that some of us assume that our children, installed in the split-level or high-rise homes we have provided, will absorb by osmosis the tolerant attitudes and new values that we have come to manifest as liberated Christian parents. Perhaps we are overlooking the simple fact that in order to play any game, one must first know the rules. I see some children carried to amusement parks more than they are to church. It is a possibility even in the South that these are the ones who were not "raised up in the way they should go" and will decamp to Hare Krishna or the Reverend

Moon; they can't all be Yankees. Are we driving them there by not providing them with an anchor that will hold in storms? What has happened to Fundamentalism? To politics?

I remember the insurgence of the Campus Crusade for Christ. To replace the mental demands of in-depth Bible study, the phenomenon of "sharing" appeared, used most often in the rather puzzling form of an intransitive verb. Legions of post-adolescents descended on the Protestant churches of the South to "share" with us and before us on Sunday mornings. They came from colleges large and small, and they came with superficial information, but an ebullient commitment to evangelism. They stood in our pulpits, bright-eyed and beautiful, smiling like jack-o'-lanterns, and prated of finding happiness in the Lord through "sharing." They consistently misquoted Revelations, and they substituted enthusiasm for knowledge but, oh Lord, they were dedicated. I regarded them as the renascence of Fundamentalism. One of our local preachers gave up his pulpit to "share" with sinners in Full Time Christian Golf. I was bewildered. Many learned ministers, solid and concerned scholars of theology and the Christian ethic, were chagrined when young people, under the spell of the Campus Crusade, departed their family churches in droves, as unthinkingly and carefree as the laughing children who followed Browning's ratkiller beyond the walls of Hamelin.

In the train of economic excess, hard on the heels of the Campus Crusade, my home was invaded by television and its preachers with their electronic exhortations for love offerings. Television teaches one to value action above dialogue, to watch rather than to think. Marketing experts, I am told, assess the mental level of the average viewer and gear programs to that level. Nowhere is this more obvious than in the fraternity of the TV evangelists. The hawk-eyed prophet, the emaciated zealot, has been replaced by ecclesiastical Thespians, plump, pious, blow-dried and sartorially resplendent. The horse of the circuit rider has long since been exchanged for foreign cars or even private planes. I watch these accomplished actors and wonder if God has not finally become inextricably confused in the Southern mind with Mammon.

From TV donations, Oral Roberts built a university in Oklahoma to the glory of God, but everybody in Fayette County, Georgia, knows that he named it after Oral. Ernest Angley pranced before the cameras with falsetto cries of "Heal" and "Ba-be" that made Mary Baker Eddy look minor league. Jim and Tammy Bakker performed so spellbindingly that it was only later one realized they have given new depth to the promise that "I come that you should have life more abundantly." I held the cloak and watched as Jimmy Swaggart fell from grace. So to speak. The tribe of Levi was besmirched.

The South was above all this, I thought, because so many of us laugh at these people. We believe in conversion still, but we think it should be personal, an intensely private experience. When politicians make much in print or on TV of the very sacred condition of having been Born Again, most of us put our tongues in cheek and feel that someone should check the placenta. Carefully.

The new Fundamentalists whom we deride are a powerful group and strive to expand that power. About ten years ago in my county, they distributed with the zeal of a holy war a list of questions to the candidates for local office. The answers, they vowed, would be printed in the local paper so that Fayette County Christians could vote with spiritual enlightenment and glorify God with their political choices. The list contained queries about blood atonement, belief in Jesus Christ as supreme ruler, prayer, homosexuality, foreign policy, literal interpretation of Scripture, and secular humanism. The list caused quite a twitter and was distributed by people calling themselves the Moral Majority. The two ladies who visited me assumed that morality did not encompass bigotry and prejudice but was restricted to adultery, an activity in which, I privately thought, it would have been almost inconceivable that either of them would have been pressured to participate. The group they represented was vociferous but not a majority; the candidates who ignored the questionnaire received more votes than the placating politicians who answered it. My faith in our local electorate was restored. We appeared politically progressive, intelligent, superior to emotional theology. There are many newcomers in Fayette County, but few of them, I assured myself, rode in on a turnip truck, and each of them was born at least the day before yesterday.

The intellectual pinnacle I fancied we had attained has not, however, been a tranquil one, uplifted and serene. I recently witnessed an imbroglio among the Baptists of our state. Some years ago, the more reactionary members of this great denomination began calling themselves "Conservatives" instead of "Fundamentalists."

I cannot remember if, in the name of trendy semantics, this was before we all had to begin saying "mobile home" instead of "trailer," but it was well after "tourist courts" became "motels" and "the Colored" became "Blacks." The conservative Baptists had wrested political control from the moderates at the state convention and installed their own officers. I watched as they sought political dominion over the largest Baptist school in the state, Mercer University in Macon. They assailed its system of trustee selection, the appearance in *Playboy* of two misguided coeds who had obviously not been raised right, and the printing in the campus newspaper of "lewd and sexually explicit" material and condom ads. They then attacked the president of Mercer, the consecrated theologian and educator, Kirby Godsey, by charging him with heresy.

Heresy in the Sovereign State of Georgia in 1987! The accusation was triggered by a series of spiritually challenging addresses on grace delivered by Dr. Godsey. A few sentences and phrases were plucked out of the tantalizing imbricate of those lectures and presented as proof that their author was heretical in his views on salvation. The assault was led by a plump little businessman with a roached-up hairdo who would not have recognized grace had he met her head on in a loan shark's office. He demanded the dismissal of Godsey and a restructuring of the board of trustees to bring it under the control of the Georgia Baptist Convention.

Well, come to find out, the everyday Baptists of Georgia who were able to love their Lord and still accept their fellow man were also able to distinguish quite clearly between a power grab and a holy war. Crying "academic freedom" and "intellectual independence," that priesthood of true believers, those beautiful Baptist moderates, clashed head on into the Conservatives with enough delegates not only to smite them hip and thigh but also to slap their wrists. They dethroned the state president and replaced him with an annealing moderate. One of the great schools in America was saved from sliding back into the Dark Ages; mind was still the mistress of man. I heard the Conservatives, on their part, depart the convention with the puzzling Christian threat, "Just wait till next year!"

Are they trounced? I do not dare to believe it. The influence of Fundamentalism is still strong in the South. Despite protestations to the contrary, we are all tarred with the Fundamentalist brush. Regardless of the intellectual superiority that some of us may feel, the one toward the other, we still have the same roots, and they are bedded in rock. They reach down into the graveyards of Georgia and are succored by the bones of our grandfathers.

This is Bible country. We support the state of Israel because we subconsciously regard the book of Exodus as a quitclaim deed to the Middle East; anything that can possibly be called Canaan belongs irretrievably to the Jews. It says so in the Bible.

Gary Hart did not stand a chance in Fayette County because not only did he dare to chisel Number VII most unrepentantly from the Decalogue but he further flouted our mores by violating what cynics call Number XI, which reads,

"Thou shalt not get caught." His petulant cries that several presidents would not have been in the White House had adultery been a criterion are only partially true. Had the news media been as candid as they are now, as clinically open in their publicity, he is correct: The South would have been informed in time for political history to have been changed. Why does he think the political future of the fat Kennedy is now confined so rigidly to Massachusetts?

Fundamentalism is the only force that has made it possible for two preachers even to be considered for the presidency. Neither has had any experience at all in government. Both are gifted in exhortation and emotionalism, however, and cavalierly destroy any barriers between church and state. One even consistently flaunts "Reverend" before his name on TV and in the papers. We think of Iran under its leader and hope that our preachers will be rebuffed by principles of Scripture; there is the clear admonition in the Bible for the shoemaker to stick to his last. It is phrased succinctly as, "Each of us has gifts. He who can preach, let him preach." I have heard it voiced locally as "Neither one them preachers got any more business in the White House than a sow hog has with a side saddle."

Fundamentalism touches us all. So does politics. Despite the irritation one feels toward labels, we are still a civilization in which the majority of our people is moral. In Georgia, that morality stems from the Holy Bible. In my county, it has its roots in the Old Testament and the Ten Commandments. The leaves, the blossom, the fruit may vary, but the roots are ever the same. The rural South believes in "Turn ye." It believes that "A remnant shall return." We in Fayette County still believe the Bible is the greatest single collection of books compiled under one cover. We believe that it should be read; it should be studied. How much of it should be believed without question is an individual matter. Some of us regard the Old Testament as a revered record of many men in their search for

God. Others of us believe the credits in the frontispiece and insist that Moses personally wrote the Pentateuch — with a goose-quill pen. Whatever. All of us where I live believe something about it. We guide our lives by it, including political decisions.

If we study with enough personal diligence instead of accepting predigested opinions about The Book, we might follow the progress of man's relationship with God and arrive beyond the rules carved in stone to the commandments imprinted on the warm human heart. We might be able to accept ourselves and all others around us as manifestations of God's image, and we might love one another and forgive one another. Unconditionally and repeatedly. We might even come to the realization that the assurance of our salvation does not depend on the fact that we believe in God, but on the surety that God believes in us. "Ye shall know the truth and the truth shall set you free."

Politics lives and thrives, but let us not forget that, in the South, religious fundamentalism still has a profound influence on it. Nobody liked Ronald Reagan except a majority of the American people.

Read. Study. *Progress* and *prosperity* are not synonyms. Mammon lives, but we do not have to bow the knee before him. Treasures yet exist that moth and rust do not corrupt. Let us seek them out; let us bequeath those treasures to our children.

I think back to a long time ago; I remember my grandfather, and I flip off the TV set. With the gesture, the evangelists fade away, retreating through a pinpoint into a wooden box fronted by an opaque rectangle. So do Tom Brokaw and Sam Donaldson.

Read, brother, read!

Then go and vote. ∎

Emily Ellison

Born on a Friday the thirteenth in July 1951 in Dalton, Georgia, Emily Ellison moved to Greenville, South Carolina, and then to a series of Southern communities before attending high school in Fort Lauderdale, Florida. She was a sharp observer who found writing easy. But she poured most of her creative energy into the visual arts, her major at the University of Georgia, until the mid-seventies when she began profiling artists and authors for a newspaper in Fairhope, Alabama. Through meetings with other writers there, she sharpened her skills and published her first novel, Alabaster Chambers *in 1979. With her second novel,* First Light, *she joined the region's emergent ranks of new and talented authors. The story of a small-town Georgian and her family, the novel richly weaves a tapestry of tension and strain, love and commitment that is unfurled as family members confront the realities of their relationships. Poet David Bottoms compared it to the works of other first-rate Southern authors who prove blood is thicker than philosophy. Ms. Ellison, who was a reporter for* The Atlanta Constitution, *also co-edited* Our Mutual Room: Modern Literary Portraits of the Opposite Sex. *Her next novel,* The Picture Maker, *is in its final stages. Winner of the 1987 Atlanta Mayor's Fellowship in the Arts for literature, she recently became a mother, leading her to new perspectives on the fabric of family life in the region.* ■

The Family: Growing Up
A Democrat

*I*t is 1960. I am nine years old, in the fourth grade, living with my mother and father in Wake Forest, North Carolina. My boyfriend this year is a handsome fellow fourth-grader by the name of Dickie Brewer. When Dickie rides his bike across town to my house, he impresses me with many things, among them his golf swing. He shows me how to lace fingers together to create a formidable grip, and he practices teeing off by hitting pine cones with a broom handle. This is something. There are no golfers in my family, only softball players and horseshoe throwers, and even as a nine-year-old, I understand that the Brewers are different from us. My hard-working father would never dream of playing golf. When we go on vacation, we visit relatives back in Georgia, or maybe spend a few days in a Florida beach motel in Panama City or Daytona, or sleep in a pop-up tent beside some cold stony creek in the mountains. When Dickie's family goes on vacation, they stay near the North Carolina golf courses at Pinehurst and Southern Pines. Dickie is smooth-skinned and tanned, the best-looking boy in my class. I have read of love, and I am pretty sure that is what this is.

There is only one problem. Dickie is a Nixon man. And I am a Kennedy woman.

Members of my family are Democrats, a fact of life as basic as the fact that we are Methodists — the non-drinking kind, who attend church twice every Sunday — and John Fitzgerald Kennedy is our candidate this year. Despite his being Catholic (I've never met a Catholic, and I know only one little Jewish girl), my parents believe he is a great man, and they are voting for him for president. I sit cross-legged on the floor in the den with them and watch Mr. Kennedy debate Mr. Nixon on TV the way children twenty years later will watch a miniseries. And after I go to bed, I hear Mother and Daddy talking down the hall for hours about what was said. I fall asleep to words such as *Eisenhower* and *Checkers* and *Massachusetts.* I hear Mother say *Jackie,* and she makes the word sound like magic.

The next day at school, my class is divided. At recess, there are slurs shouted back and forth about both JFK and Richard Nixon. It gets nasty, and I am forced to take sides. I am not exactly sure *why* I am a Democrat and why more than half of my classmates are Republicans. But the differences in our two candidates seem to me as distinct as the fact that on Saturdays, while Dickie and his father play golf, Daddy and I get dirty pulling honeysuckle and poison ivy out of the back yard. I also notice that the boys who are always missing from school several weeks every spring and fall, helping their families sow and harvest crops, are the ones who side with me for John Kennedy; a boy named Douglas, whose hands have turned a rusty color from working with his dad on their dairy farm, has begun sending me intricately folded notes expressing his allegiance to me and the Yankee senator. But it seems several of my girlfriends, whose fathers work at the seminary, are mostly siding with Dickie for this Nixon fellow.

Dickie Brewer is one heck of a looker, but because I am loyal to my party (i.e. my parents), I just don't think we can work things out. I have the suspicion that very soon he will give up on me and start pedaling it over to Laurie Duncan's house. But what is love when compared to politics?

Ella Pangle Jordan turned ninety years old on November 22, 1987. Until fifteen years ago, she was taking daily jogs around the yard — not a flat-out run, but not a stroll, either. Today she still gets her exercise: She dresses in purple warmup suits, she plays a mean game of Scrabble and her passions are baseball and politics. Nannie, as my grandmother is called, is a Democrat. One of the most emphatic in the family.

Recently, a woman at church thought she was paying Nannie a compliment when she said, "You know, you look just like Nancy."

My grandmother was confused. "Nancy?" she said.

"Sure," the woman told her. "Nancy Reagan." It must have been the look Nannie gave her, because the woman slowly backed off and said, "Oh, I guess I've said the wrong thing."

Nannie likes to tell you that Nancy Reagan is so skinny she'd get sucked into the updraft of one of those presidential helicopters if it weren't for that dog at the end of the leash holding her down. She doesn't like Nancy's husband, either. Or nearly any other Republican you can mention. In fact, she'll get hot in the face if you mention any to whom you have slight loyalties. Some in the family won't even talk politics with her anymore because she gets so angry; my father usually leaves the room if Reagan shows up on TV and Nannie is present.

There's something puzzling though: As adamant as Nannie is about her politics, the woman has never voted. Not once in any political election. Not once in all these ninety years.

I learned my politics by watching those Kennedy-Nixon debates with my parents; by falling asleep in the back seat of a '59 Plymouth while listening to their discussions about Adlai Stevenson and Lyndon Johnson and Hubert Humphrey; by having my father read not children's books to me every night before bed but the biographies of those men he thought were great: King David, Abraham Lincoln, Gandhi. He admired, I learned, men who were self-made, honest, straight-talking and who worked in the service of common people.

I always assumed my parents' politics were their own. I

don't know why I was so late in learning that, like me, my parents were taught their politics at home. And that Nannie, the truest yellow-dog Democrat of all, began leaning left because of *her* father and mother. It probably all goes back a lot further even than William Calvin and Samantha Leonard Pangle, but that's as far back as anyone living can tell me.

The home where my great-grandparents raised their family in Georgia's Whitfield County was built in the late 1800s by a former Confederate officer, General Gordon, and was later owned by the ancestors of a Georgia congressman, Bo Callaway. The bricks that formed that house were made in a field out behind the home site, from red Georgia clay. In that same field, they were baked in a fire that never reached the temperatures of a modern-day kiln. Today I own one of those bricks, and each time I go to dust under it, there is a fine reddish-orange powder where, because of the improper heat at which it was baked, it has disintegrated a little further.

These few bricks that some of us in the family have, and those bits and pieces that are now piled in a rubble on that same piece of land where they were made, are all that is left of W.C. Pangle's house. It is gone now, first pulled at by the hands of a tornado during the sixties and then yanked down the rest of the way by man.

But at the time my great-grandfather reigned there, it stood at the edge of a country dirt road just west of Dalton, Georgia. It was a fine house then, with white cotton curtains blowing in and out the screenless windows, with rocking chairs lining the porches and with enough wide, high rooms to rear eight children. I've heard stories about all those children at one time or another. But the ones who gave me stories of their own, the ones from whom I learned the most about our family's political history, were Nannie; her youngest brother, Tom Pangle; and their sister Allie's son, Donald MacArthur.

Great-grandfather Pangle was, according to all three, the one who gave political cues not only to his own children and grandchildren but to almost everyone else in the area. He was a reader, they told me, and rows of law books lined his shelves; he was also the only one for miles around who took the three-times-a-week *Atlanta Constitution.* "I never did know of nobody else taking that paper back then," my eighty-two-year-old Uncle Tom tells me today. "He did more reading up on things than anyone else."

It was, therefore, William Calvin Pangle — a farmer, sawmiller, owner of a country store and justice of the peace — who, because he was listened to, was the kind of man state and local politicians scouted out and courted. They knew if they had his vote, they also had the vote of nearly everyone else in the county.

And, like most rural folks in Georgia in those days, it was Eugene Talmadge for whom W.C. Pangle said to vote. Even as adults, according to Uncle Tom, he and his brothers never disagreed with their daddy's decisions. Red-gallused Gene Talmadge may have been "a mean old devil," but Tom and the other Pangle boys voted him in as governor anyway; and later they voted for old Gene's son, Herman. It was Herman, after all, who convinced his father to lower the price of Georgia's car tags to three dollars. "He told him, 'Lots of those working people can't pay twelve and fifteen dollars.'"

In the days of the three-dollar car tag, young Tom Pangle often drove local folks to drop their ballots in the Whitfield County Courthouse or over at Mount Vernon School. "A Talmadge worker would pick out a man who knew the community," Uncle Tom tells me, "and pay him to take people to go to vote. Sometimes they'd include a bottle of whiskey with the pay." Mostly, though, it was only *men* who rode in my uncle's car. "I've hauled some women to vote," he says. "But that was after I was grown." It was also only "us boys" who gathered around my great-grandfather at his McCutheon's Cross Roads store and listened to what he had read in the *Constitution* and discussed with politicians.

But what about the women? Those four Pangle daughters? Ella, Annie, Allie, and Cora certainly had their political opinions, and there has been mention of even a rift or two among the siblings, particularly when "the girls" didn't want Al Smith to be elected president because he was against Prohibition. I've even heard it whispered that one year Annie wasn't for Talmadge. But if all of them had such strong political notions, why is it that at least one of the daughters has gone her entire life without having voted?

It has only been in this election year that I have had a guess at why.

Nannie's baby brother Tom is a widower now, who lives alone except for his dog, Rock. Most any day you drive up in front of his house in Dalton, you're likely to find him out in the yard with Rock, splitting wood; or he'll be inside by the fire spitting tobacco juice in a can, reading a Western or a detective novel. He also gets in his little white pickup truck almost every day and drives down to the corner to get his copy of the *Constitution.* If he's going much farther than the store or into town, he gets a younger friend of his (who's only seventy-five) to drive, and once a week, they head out to the west side of Dalton to visit his nephew, Donald MacArthur.

Tom and Nannie's second-oldest sister, Allie, married Houston Parks MacArthur in the early part of this century. Her young husband's family was related to Sam Houston and had moved down to Georgia from South Carolina. He and Aunt Allie had two sons, H.P. and Donald. H.P. was a Whitfield County school superintendent and the local sheriff. Donald also served as sheriff, was elected mayor of Dalton for one term back in the 1940s and for a while was vice chairman of the Democratic Party in his northwest Georgia district. Their father had been the county commissioner.

Today, at seventy, Donald cares as much about politics as he did when he was mayor, and he still keeps up with the issues as devoutly as ever. On a recent Sunday afternoon visit, the first thing he tells me is that he has been watching a TV program about one of the presidential candidates. He also reminds me that later in the evening there is going to be a televised debate among the Republican candidates. I tell him my preference among the contenders in this election, and he says, "Good. You're a Democrat."

My cousin Donald's love of politics, like the rest of ours, goes back to his grandfather, William Calvin Pangle. "He was the patriarch of the family unit," Donald says, and he, like everyone else in the family, learned his political lessons "from Grandpa's knees."

"We all listened to him. The nieces and nephews, and sons and daughters."

On this Sunday afternoon, it is one of the daughters who is puzzling me, and I tell him I've learned that Nannie has never voted. "I didn't know about Aunt Ella," Donald says with Christian concern. "I need to talk to her about that."

And then Donald gives me what I've been looking for. "I don't know of anybody except Grandmother who didn't take a hand in politics, that and Methodism. Grandmother didn't believe women should vote."

I have a photograph of Samantha Pangle's family taken when Nannie was maybe ten or eleven. The whole family is outside in front of the big redbrick house, the older sons off to themselves, leaning against one of the porches, and the grown daughters and the younger children gathered around their parents who are sitting in wicker rockers in the yard. Samantha is beside her mustached husband, holding baby Tom. Nannie is standing beside her, tall and skinny for her age, with hands held together in front of her. She looks innocent, but I've heard the stories. She once burned down the family barn, and she and her brother Gus were notorious for finding trouble. If you look closely, you get a glimpse of that daredevil personality and future sense of humor in Nannie's young face. But when you look over at the somber, high-boned face of her mother, you can tell Samantha Pangle was the type who, like her husband, would have been listened to and respected by all her children. Even feisty Ella. It seems that now, even at ninety, Nannie is listening still.

*The silhouette was made when Ms. Ellison was nine years old
and learning the differences between Democrats and Republicans.*

When the Tennessee writer John Egerton began researching his book *Generations, An American Family,* he thought it was possible to find one family of four or five living generations that typified the majority of America's middle-class families. I think the family that began with Samantha and W.C. Pangle is also typical of so many of those who have resided in the rural South for the past one hundred years. In Ecclesiastes it is written, "One generation passes away, and another generation comes, but the earth abides forever." In the solid South, for a long time, it appeared as if the Democratic Party would abide forever. My family was not unusual in that its members raised their children, as they had been raised, at the breast of that party.

In this election year, I gave birth to my first child. When the Democratic Party's convention came to Atlanta, she was six months old. Only the very oldest members of her family now fully support that party and its nominees without question — those such as Nannie and Tom and Donald. The rest of us, spread as we are across the country, have strayed some from both the church and the party our forefathers were raised in. My own brother, a decade younger than I, once headed the Republican Party on his college campus (Nannie and I just couldn't talk about it), and even my parents started siding, bit by bit, with him and Ronald Reagan.

The South that once voted a straight Democratic ticket no longer exists. According to my great-uncle, it was economic reasons that led his father and nearly every other rural Southerner to be Democrats. "Southerners didn't have any business being Republicans because they didn't have any money," says Uncle Tom. Southerners were poor, farmers mostly, who voted for the likes of Eugene Talmadge because "he wouldn't lie to you and he paid his debts."

Today the South is no longer so poor. Or agrarian. And politics are no longer the main topic of interest as they were when Uncle Tom, his brothers and their neighbors gathered in my great-grandfather's store; and being involved in politics doesn't even occur to most of us as it did in my cousin Donald's day when "you weren't very patriotic if you didn't participate."

The lack of interest has to do, in part, as Donald MacArthur believes, with the fact that there are so many more things to occupy most of us today. But there's also this: A person who reads today's newspapers with the same enthusiasm as my great-grandfather does not come away with the same amount of knowledge. The issues of his day were more clearly defined. Today, though, when you've read everything you can about Nicaragua, do you truly know what to believe? How do you begin to fight racism that continues even after the doors have been opened at offices and schools? How do you know what to do about the disappearance of the ozone layer? Where are you going to dump all that toxic waste? How do you get involved without looking like Amy Carter?

When I was pregnant with Ellison Fletcher Perry, among the other usual numerous fears of a soon-to-be mother, I worried about her future politics. I worried about such a seemingly irrational thing because I see all around me a generation coming of age that is far more conservative than the generation that raised them.

Daily now, though, I remind myself that two people's definitions of happiness are hardly ever the same, and I try not to be too neurotic about the thought of my daughter as a possible Republican. (Her own father, after all, is a golfer; though most times, he votes the way he's supposed to.) Whatever her political leanings, I feel certain she'll grow up learning two things: that the political process itself greatly matters and that, no matter how complicated the issues, it's important to keep trying to figure them out. She'll have not only me and her father to thank or blame for that, but several generations of reading Democrats who came before her.

From my family have come mayors (including Katharine Robinson of Metter, who was one of the first women mayors in Georgia), school superintendents, county commissioners and an awful lot of voters. Many of those people, along with most of my ancestors, are buried up on a hill in Whitfield County. I visited that hill not long ago and listened to the wind shaking the branches of an oak tree and scooting by the grave markers with a noise like a sweet human whistle. I was hoping I'd hear more — maybe Samantha or Calvin or Cora or Allie telling me something.

If I could have, I would have told them something, too, particularly my great-grandfather. I'd like him to know that, so many decades and generations after him, I once worked as a reporter for that newspaper he so loved. I'd like him to know that I, too, daily read that paper, and *The New York Times,* with the same appetite for political news he had; I'd like him to know that all these elections later, my husband, Chuck Perry, published Herman Talmadge's autobiography and we have been in that man's home and seen firsthand a framed set of famous red suspenders. I'd like him to know that in all the world, the place I'd most like to be is out on the road covering one of the political candidates, sitting in some greasy diner somewhere in the Midwest or New England or the Deep South, smoking cigarettes and drinking coffee, talking to the locals and asking other reporters the question my friend Celestine Sibley always asks, "What do you hear?"

But in this election year, the year my child was born, I'd like most of all to see my ninety-year-old grandmother finally registered to vote. I'd like to go with Nannie when she casts her ballot for the first time, too. And when we go, I'm enough of a romantic that I'd like it to be my great-uncle Tom who drives us to the polls. ■

Roy Reed

Just as barbecue and pepper sauces have spiced Southern cooking, colorful characters of all stripes have added flavor to its political life, and it is that question of character that fascinates Roy Reed. Now professor of journalism at the University of Arkansas, he began his career at the Arkansas Gazette *before joining* The New York Times *in 1965 as a Southern correspondent based in Atlanta. "Selma was in the news then, and Dr. King and George Wallace," recalls Reed, who covered civil rights, politics and rural affairs before winding up his fourteen-year career with the newspaper nine years ago in London. From his campus office, Reed continues to keep a close watch on the South, and when the spirit moves, he writes essays, book reviews and articles from his hill-country cattle farm in Hogeye, Arkansas. Last year, for example, he lofted a few notions on television in the Ozarks for* TV Guide. *"The piece suggested that getting television signals into the hollers was more trouble than it was worth," Reed says. "You would have thought I had sacked a church. The TV people around here are still howling. But the main value of essay writing is that you can do it at your own desk in your own time. I see it as a reward for twenty-five years of bad food, bad motels, bad airplanes and abusive politicians." Reed's critically acclaimed collection of essays,* Looking for Hogeye, *was published by the University of Arkansas Press in 1986.* ■

The Southern Demagogue: Death of a Breed

ecil Roberts of Birmingham, who has followed and improved Alabama politics for a generation, sounded stumped.

"I don't think there are any demagogues at all in Alabama now," she said. "I'll ask around."

No demagogues left in Alabama? But that amazing and historic condition is not the half of it. In an exhaustive survey of the old Confederacy, conducted as the sap was rising this spring and politics was approaching the boil, not a single Southern demagogue of national stature could be found. Not one, at least, cast in the old mold.

Something historic has happened. Not only is demagoguery on the ropes, but there has been a general blanding of the politics of the South. The region that gave us Senator Claghorn is now electing Ivy League governors and senators. Members of the new breed speak economics as a second language. They take speech classes to learn how to raise their voices.

The changed public character of Southern officeholders apparently dates to the onslaught of television as a political tool. The change gathered momentum with the defusing of race as the region's great issue and finally came to a head in the late seventies about the time that George Wallace, who was once the best demagogue in Alabama or anywhere else, emerged as a Christian and announced that he had become an integrationist.

The overriding reason for it all seems to be the changed nature of what was once the nation's most distinctive region. Ratcheting to match the nation's rising scorn, the level of flamboyance in the South's public figures rose spectacularly during the decades before the crash — the crash of racism as a formula for winning elections, the crash of defiant eccentricity as a defense against the great outside and the final crash of proud, beloved isolation when America's most inward-looking region agreed to rejoin the Union.

It is tempting to say that the South is no longer purely Southern. I am not willing to go that far, but I do believe that as the region has lost much of its racial bias and at the same time has shifted from countrified to citified and developed a taste for *60 Minutes,* fast food and Ronald Reagan, there is simply no longer much profit in *acting* purely Southern. That change in posture can be seen clearly in the men and women Southerners now elect to high office. The typical Southern politician of the late eighties would look as much at home in Hartford and Minneapolis as in Atlanta and Little Rock.

Not only that: As the region has been drawn into the national culture, a funny thing has happened. The nation has been drawn into the Southern culture. Like an occupation army on foreign soil, the United States is taking on Southern tastes in food, music and public attitudes. The Nashville twang has corrupted the Yankee airwaves, and a Southern kind of politics has spread to the Canadian border and the two oceans. Does anyone doubt that there is a serious connection between Jesse Jackson's national popularity (or Pat Robertson's, for that matter) and the fact that Cajun food and fried catfish are now served in the restaurants of New York City?

I can think of only one exception to the general sweep of this phenomenon. The careful reader will notice that I have referred to the disappearance of Southern demagogues *of national stature.* That reference is not mere semantics.

But first, what are the reasons for the drabbing of Dixie's

political landscape? A generation ago, the South owned practically all of the American irregulars, the men of true and extreme talent who were able to push their notoriety beyond their own state borders. There were, besides Governor Wallace, Orval E. Faubus of Arkansas; Earl K. Long, Jimmie Davis, Willie Rainach and Leander Perez, all of Louisiana; Ross Barnett of Mississippi; "Bull" Connor and Jim Clark of Alabama; Lester Maddox of Georgia, and (the young) Strom Thurmond of South Carolina. Anyone over the age of forty can add names to that list without effort.

With the exceptions of Earl Long, who declined to demagogue the race issue, and Jimmie Davis, who was always more of an entertainer than a politician, every man on the list made his national reputation as a segregationist. And therein lies a large reason for the declining volatility of Southern politics. The fate of racial politics was sealed with the national civil rights legislation of the sixties. (It is of no small interest, I think, that the laws most responsible for changing the face of the South were enacted under the lash of the much-scorned Southerner Lyndon B. Johnson.) When politics was a white pastime in the South, race was the main fuel of the old flame-throwers. Now that blacks participate, the political language and rules have changed.

Racial demagogues have disappeared not because of any great moral improvement in the South. They have gone because they are no longer needed to incite The Issue and keep the fearful millions in debt to their dark fantasies. If blacks by some calamity were to lose the vote again, white demagogues would find employment once more.

I said earlier that Earl Long was not one of those demagogues who used race to make his reputation. He not only failed to profit from the issue, he actually spent lavishly of his political capital to avoid exploiting it. It was during a debate over racist politics that the old man lost his hold on what his handlers deemed reality. His wife shipped him to an insane asylum. His memory deserves to have it repeated that he was on the floor of the Louisiana Legislature opposing racist legislation when his breakdown occurred.

Going crazy over politics was always most likely to happen in Louisiana, the South's political extremity. Political theater has been part of the Louisiana scene from the beginning. There was once a shooting war on Canal Street in New Orleans, with Creoles on one side and "Americans" on the other, blazing away at each other, and massed citizens in the rear, uptown and downtown, cheering their champions on. When Judge Leander Perez announced that he would imprison all incoming civil rights agitators on a Mississippi River island that everyone knew was inhabited by alligators and cottonmouth moccasins, citizens reacted as they would have at a play — with whistles, applause and groans of outrage.

Huey and Earl Long were the Shakespeare and Marlowe of their state. Some say that Edwin Edwards, who left the Louisiana governor's office this spring, to be succeeded by a correct and thoughtful Harvard man, was the last of the South's flamboyant politicians. The argument goes that if excess is finished in Louisiana, the most indulgent culture in the nation, there can be no doubt that the tradition of Gene Talmadge, Theodore Bilbo, James K. Vardaman and "Cotton Ed" Smith is dead.

Let us examine the proposition. Was Edwin Edwards, the gambler, womanizer, cohort of shady practitioners, freewheeler, and, just incidentally, Louisiana's most progressive governor since Earl Long, truly the end of a Southern tradition?

He might have been. On the question of women, for example, no modern Southern politician save a lone hombre from Texas (about whom more later) has actually cultivated a reputation for skirt-chasing. There are probably several dozen among the new quiet, cleaned-up, Americanized breed who take pains to obscure their dalliances, but Mr. Edwards talks openly of the matter. We have not seen his like since James E. "Kissin' Jim" Folsom of Alabama in the years after World War II. Governor Folsom, a rustic progressive who

As the setting has shifted from outdoors on the courthouse lawns to indoors in the television studios, Reed says, a 'general blanding of the politics of the South' has occurred.

disturbed the establishment, was once quoted as saying, "If my political enemies think they can catch ol' Jim by getting some pretty young thing, putting a nice dress on her, and reeling her by in front of Big Jim — if they think they can catch ol' Jim that way, they're right.... They're gonna catch Jim every time."

When Governor Edwards and a leader of the Legislature were caught flying to Las Vegas to gamble, the legislator, who lived in the Bible Belt of northern Louisiana, issued a statement asking forgiveness and vowing never to do it again. The governor, a Cajun from the Lowcountry, called a press conference and talked about his winnings. He said he liked to gamble and intended to return to Las Vegas every chance he got. The voters improved his margin of victory in the next election by several percentage points.

But for all his resemblance to the hot-blooded freebooters of the past, Edwin Edwards in one important way is more in tune with the new wave of Southern politicians than with the old. I am thinking of the vital area of style.

Contrast Mr. Edwards' style with that of Earl Long. While Mr. Edwards moves with fast company, Mr. Long preferred low. Mr. Edwards likes class in his women. Mr. Long picked up stripteasers on Bourbon Street. Mr. Edwards buys his champagne from French chateaux and drinks it in the best restaurants of Paris. Mr. Long got his for two dollars a bottle and guzzled it in the honky-tonk cantinas of Juarez.

In language, the best indication of style, Earl Long was closer to Chaucer than to Edwin Edwards. Here is an excerpt from Governor Long's speech to the Legislature on the day he lost his balance. Listen to the poetry. Listen to the unabashed excess:

"Before I'd sell out the people of this state, before I'd make them poor old colored people an issue, and have people hatin' 'em and fightin' 'em and burnin' their houses down, I'd sacrifice being president of the United States, vice president or United States senator!"

Here he was on another occasion, bludgeoning an opponent: "He's in every skin game he can get in. And he's baldheaded!"

And here again, speaking of a wealthy young opponent with social pretensions: "I think a good beating would do him more good than anything on Earth. I think it'd help his wife, and help his father, help his mother, help everybody. And I think it'd just let him know that some things don't grow on trees; you can't just reach up and get it. Because he's a hothouse plant. He was born with a silver spoon in his mouth, and you couldn't get it out with a crowbar."

Now listen to Mr. Edwards skewering a lumbering, dull opponent during the 1983 election campaign: "It takes him an hour and a half to watch *60 Minutes*."

That was all — a single deft thrust. Earl Long would have choked on such a compression of his wit. But the one-liner, as Mr. Edwards and the new Southern leaders understand, is now as common in the Sun Belt as in the Snow Belt. National television brought it south. *60 Minutes* has taken the place of Sunday night church services for millions of Southerners. When a Louisiana governor utters a one-liner, the voters get it.

There was a small, ignoble moment in the sixties that foreshadowed the new technological reality that, along with the death of racial demagoguery, was to change forever the way the Southern voters perceived their political leaders. Big Jim Folsom was not the only Southern politician to take a drink, but he was the first to appear drunk on television. The moment was more historic than Governor Folsom or any other Southern politician understood at the time. The night before the 1962 Democratic primary, he appeared on live television so drunk that he could not remember his children's names as he tried to introduce them. Thousands of viewers watched and judged. He lost the primary to George Wallace. That moment on television effectively ended his career.

What Big Jim and few other Southerners of the time realized was the awesome power of the televised image. Until then, a politician could fairly safely assume that his action in one context would not be judged against his word in another. A candidate for governor of Arkansas could promise a paved road to the voters of Harrison in the northern Ozarks one day, and then make the same promise the next day, using the same appropriation of money and changing only the geography of the road, across the state in El Dorado.

Context was not the only thing affected by television. A politician's behavior, demeanor, credibility, salability — his whole public persona — had to change with the advent of the new medium.

I spent much of the 1964 political season on a succession of courthouse lawns watching Orval Faubus run for his sixth term as governor of Arkansas. His opponent was Winthrop Rockefeller, a scion of the famous oil empire. Mr. Faubus told the same anecdote at every stop. As a boy, it was his job to walk beside the family wagon and carry the newly bought jug of kerosene back to the farm. They couldn't risk carrying it in the wagon. Some might slosh out. The stuff was precious, he thundered, because old John D. Rockefeller, the grandfather of this upstart Winthrop, had cornered the market and raised the price so high that poor people could barely afford to buy it. Fifty years had passed, but the outrage seemed fresh in the face of every farmer in Mr. Faubus' audiences.

I cannot picture that scene on television. Quite apart from the problem of repetition (one telling on the air and the story is used up), the basic presumptions of the two media are in opposition. The medium of the courthouse lawn caters to hot oratory and the intense messenger. Sweat needs to be produced on both sides of the podium. What we now so readily call demagoguery was actually a natural extension of the Southern landscape.

The platform of communication has now shifted indoors to rooms called studios. The crowds are the cameramen and technicians. The new medium calls for neckties, pressed shirts and the appearance of reasonableness. Sweat is no longer an aid to communication; it is a makeup problem.

There is more. Before television, the politician was presented to the absent voter by newspaper. A newspaper report of a speech is not the whole speech but a compression of its main themes. The reporter fills in the setting, the crowd, and the speaker's style and demeanor. What the reader got, before television, was the essence of the event. In the case of a master communicator such as Bilbo or Gene Talmadge, what the reader got was a very strong essence, even on the printed page.

The television viewer cannot take the place of the reporter, selecting the colorful, just-right quotations to spice up the report, reducing the thirty-minute speech to the two or three main themes, summarized in a few words. Nor can he add descriptive touches or insert history and background to put the remarks in perspective. The reporter's task in the age of television has to be performed to a large degree by the politician himself. On television, Michael Dukakis, Jesse Jackson and George Bush must see to it that the viewer gets the intended impression, complete with nuance and background noise. Since modern Southerners tend to speak more or less standard English, that means that the Southern politician must not only perform the reporter's work but do it with a minimum of linguistic flourish. And since the modern Southerner has Americanized a lot of his tastes, the new politician must not appear too intense, angry or earthy in his role as reporter and communicator.

Even a little honest hyperbole is risky. Every word uttered by the television politician must sound reasonable to the reasonable viewer. The political message delivered on television is aimed at the sane man and woman in the audience, the citizen sitting quietly in his living room unsurrounded by any noisy crowd stirring up the blood, sitting quietly and ready to be affronted by excess — the same excess that he might applaud and yell for more of if he were standing in a crowd on a hot summer night in a courthouse square.

We have about used up our supply of romance in Southern politics. Anatole Broyard, who learned to think in New Orleans, wrote recently in *The New York Times Book Review,* "Democracy, which is against all sorts of excesses but its own, seems to fear romanticism as a perpetuation of inequalities and a penchant for suffering." Mr. Broyard says that the minimalism so popular in today's literature may be a defense against romanticism. The South seems to be joining the national rebellion against romanticism. In politics, as in literature, little is ventured. The new political language of America is meager and bland, and the South is learning to speak it. Dixie sends its children to the Ivy League, and they return instructing us in the unromantic arts of development, economics and educational standards. Irrationally, these ideas sound good on television. But they have little room for stretch and flexibility in the imagination of the audience.

The old guys tried television. Faubus, Wallace, Maddox, Barnett — they all went on television and peddled their doctrines. They should have asked Jim Folsom first. What they learned to their sorrow was that the segregationist pose had a very limited appeal on television. The same air waves that carried the pose from Montgomery to Selma also carried it to Michigan, Vermont and California — and to the black side of town in Montgomery and Selma. Those televised images galvanized the opposition to the Southern Way of Life. As the civil rights movement was electrified, Congress felt the shock. Laws were passed, and the Way of Life was swept into history. Thus were the two currents joined, the new communications medium and the new biracial politics. Excess was doomed.

Or so it seemed. Before we leave the subject, I have to share the other results of my spring survey on demagoguery. It is true that almost no demagogues of national stature are left (Jesse Helms and his red scare are becoming a bore), but it turns out that we still have small pockets of demagoguery right across the Confederacy.

In the lower levels of nearly every state — possibly excepting Mrs. Roberts' Alabama — you can still find large numbers of political scamps and bandits. They inhabit the state legislatures and city councils and county courthouses. Most will never make it into statewide office.

My state of Arkansas was amused a couple of years ago when one of our mayors left his wife and took up with a majorette. In Texas, the Legislature recently considered a counseling program for sex offenders. A member named Foster Whaley, whom the writer Molly Ivins describes as "a classic, sweet-ol'-boy," rose to protest. Ms. Ivins reported the scene as follows: "Hell with counseling 'em, quoth he, the thing to do is get out a rusty knife and whack off their, um, private parts." Mr. Whaley offered to show the warden how to do it.

Texas also sports a congressman named Charlie Wilson who got into the national news not long ago when his girlfriend, a former Miss USA, accompanied him on a tour of the front in Afghanistan. He also took her to help inspect an aircraft carrier and was huffy when the Navy made him pay her airfare.

These days, however, going to higher office usually quiets a fellow. We had a sheriff in Arkansas who made national headlines a few years ago by chaining prisoners to the gate of the state penitentiary to force the state to take them off his hands. He is now in Washington as Democratic Representative Tommy Robinson of Arkansas. He has abandoned Wyatt Earp and taken Henry Kissinger as his hero.

It is possible that the announced death of the Southern demagogue is premature. Who knows which county seat adventurer now sitting in some obscure sheriff's office might rise to the occasion if a new demand materialized? What seems more likely, though, is a long, lingering condition in which our small-bore demagogues will be nourished only by small, special constituencies.

Ferrell Guillory, who writes for the *Raleigh News and*

Observer, has been telling his readers that the nature of Southern politics has been fundamentally changed by the growing urbanization of the region. A different, quieter appeal is needed, he says, when the constituency shifts from rural to urban.

He is probably right, and one implication of that is not comforting. This year's presidential campaign offers evidence that the same currents that move the nation now move the South. Albert Gore is as much a product of Washington as of Tennessee. Pat Robertson and Jesse Jackson, Southerners with more than a little of the old taste for public theater, are national phenomena. Part of the Southern tradition has gone national. But it is not quite true to say that none of the Southern culture thrives in isolation anymore, that the parochialism that cast up Bilbo and Perez no longer exists, undiluted by national culture. Even the television satellite has not been able to obliterate the true local boys such as the knife-wielding legislator Foster Whaley and the stubborn constituencies that keep them in office. It is possible that not enough votes will survive to keep the rustic and local heroes in office much longer. If that happens, then some significant population of the rural and small-town South will be left without leaders, without heroes, without solace in their public loneliness. These leaderless people will live on for generations, raw as Indians, declining and struggling, the gorge always in the throat, scorned, rejected, despised, dangerous to the end.

Most of us Southerners, of course, have become too sophisticated for the country boys who used to lead us all. We want our politicians now to dress at Brooks Brothers and act like Episcopalians. We are ashamed of our origins. That is the kind of shame that makes us forget where we came from: that is, that we are the children of people who not only waded manure but also revered the soil; people who knew with some precision how food was created; who understood the caprices of nature and dealt at firsthand with cruelty, suffering and death, and had no Percodan to blunt their pain, no

BMW to soothe their egos, no analyst to set their lives straight, and no glistening, sanitized hospital room to ease them into eternity.

For better or worse, we have lost our grip on an important part of our heritage of style. The old redneck demagogues had swagger. Even the most colorful of our new political leaders are merely dashing. People who swap swagger for dash have an identity problem. They are having trouble remembering who they are. ■

Will D. Campbell

A National Council of Churches race relations worker aligned with leaders of the civil rights movement, the Reverend Will D. Campbell surprised many people in the sixties when he began reaching out to poor whites who seemed to be the enemies of racial progress, even venturing into Ku Klux Klan meetings and performing weddings and funerals for Klan families. Ranging forth from his farm in Mount Juliet, Tennessee, with a cherry walking stick in his hand, a broad-brimmed hat on his head and cowboy boots on his feet, the down-home Baptist preacher without a steeple has become well-known as a prophet, poet and proclaimer of a message of reconciliation rarely heard in conventional pulpits. His theology, in essence: "We're all bastards, but God loves us." The son of cotton farmers in Amite County, Mississippi, Campbell was baptized in a muddy river at age seven and ordained at seventeen but, even while claiming "redneckery" as his ancestral condition, continued with his education, earning a master's in English literature at Tulane University and a theology degree from Yale. When he is not speaking out on issues related to racial and economic justice, he serves as unofficial chaplain to the country music world in Nashville, Tennessee. Somehow, he also finds time to write. Campbell is the author of two moving memoirs, Brother to a Dragonfly *and* Forty Acres and a Goat, *as well as a novel,* The Glad River. ∎

Used and Abused: The Redneck's Lot

Bowed by the weight of centuries
He leans upon his hoe and
gazes on the ground....

dwin Markham's poem unwittingly describes my ancestors as they leaned on the hoe and gazed on the red clays of the South. In the process, they left that cervical area from the temporal bones to the first dorsal vertebra exposed to the searing, shriveling, parching rays of midday sun. *Red* necks.

Like the nouns *nigger* and *kike, redneck* is most often used pejoratively. And, as a descendant of people disparaged by that word, I ask why the first two terms are eschewed by even the most blatantly racist and bigoted publications, while *redneck* is used routinely in virtually every respectable, sophisticated and allegedly responsible newspaper and magazine in America?

Nor am I alone in such questioning. On a wall in our Mount Juliet, Tennessee, home there is an original Allen and Hatley cartoon. Two prosperous-looking men are walking out of an office building. One is black and one is white. The black man says to the white, "Here's why I worry about liberals, Lester. What do you call a poor person from Puerto Rico?"

"A Hispanic-surnamed American."

"How about an illiterate Sioux?"

"A disadvantaged native American, of course."

"And a dirt farmer of Scots-Irish ancestry?"

"A redneck, naturally."

The anamnestic rumblings in the black man's head show in his expression, a recollection of old ways and days apt to come again if the guard is lowered. He throws his hands about his head and says, "That's why I worry."

On the wall opposite this cartoon is a panel of photographs of my ancestors. Four of the pictures portray, by a dictionary's definition of redneck, "the white rural laboring class in the southern United States." Plez Webb's is the first picture. He was my great-grandfather who migrated from south of Atlanta in the late eighteenth century and homesteaded in the Mississippi territory. The picture beside his is Grandma Bettye's. She worked in the fields and kitchens, bore eleven children and died at the age of eighty-eight. Her baby son, my daddy, is featured in the third picture. He lived and labored a few rods from where he was born eighty-eight years ago. My eldest brother, who died at forty-five, is there with them.

And all of us rednecks (I speak within the camaraderie of the white ghetto, just as many black people say "nigger" within the camaraderie of the black ghetto) have become convenient scapegoats for the subtle institutionalized racism that has replaced blatant Jim Crow. In common usage, *redneck* has become synonymous with *racist* and *bigot.*

What must be understood is that *all* whites, not just rednecks, are racist because racism is the condition in and structure under which we live and move and have our being. By the accident of my white birth, I could have become president, governor, manager of a major league football team or pastor of the Roswell Street Baptist Church in Atlanta, Georgia. I live where I want. I participate in a society, every facet of which has afforded me the edge. I can change my attitudes. I can be educated out of a mind filled with hate and bigotry. But I cannot stop being a racist.

It has nothing to do with how liberal or radical or enlightened or educated or good I am. Nor does it have to do with how reactionary, conservative, ignorant or bad I am. It just has to do with *being white within these structures.* This fact subconsciously threatens most Americans, so we must go on equating racism with redneckism.

Nonetheless, I am proud of my people, because I know that historically they, too, were the victims of time, of seeds they did not plant, and the harvest of which has been thrust upon them. They could have done worse. But I know that without the incessant manipulation by the politics of the privileged, my people would have done better.

As one who has been through the romance and drama of participation in the civil rights movement, I know how easy it was, and is, to identify with the most obvious minority — in this case the blacks — and dismiss a less obvious minority — the rednecks, woolhats, peckerwoods, po' whites — as "The Enemy." But there is a real sense in which the redneck has been victimized one step beyond the black.

It is bad to have your back and your blood taken as happened to the blacks. But there is a sense in which it is worse to have your *head* taken away. Throughout their slavery, and since, the black minority knew what was happening, knew that they were suffering, knew who was causing it. And early, these blacks set about the task of doing something about it. They created a culture out of their slavery: a history complete with art, music and literature. But we whites never got their *head.* The job on the redneck was more extensive because he had his *head* taken away. He has been so thoroughly manipulated and deceived that he still hasn't identified his "Enemy."

From the beginning, you see, the redneck was the creature of the system he came to. In the beginning, and for the most part, I am convinced, the white rural laboring class in the southern United States immigrated as indentured servants. I think it is true of my own ancestors, who made their way east and south from Virginia, where Wesley Frank Craven estimated in *White, Red and Black: The 17th Century Virginia,* that seventy-five percent or more of the colony's settlers in the 1600s were servants. And these precursors of rednecks came with a dream: When their indenture was over, they would compete with their skills and energies on the open labor market in a new and developing country. "Serve me for seven years and I will set you free." But free to do what and in what context? Most often it was a freedom to flounder, to drift, to wander westward in frustrating search of what had been promised but never delivered — a secure life in a land of plenty.

I am not saying that all redneck history can be traced back to an indentured servanthood. In fact, very little of it can be so traced historically today, because white scholars have never dwelt on it. But the indications of its genesis are strong, as David W. Galenson notes in *White Servitude in Colonial America,* issued by the Cambridge University Press in 1981. Galenson quotes Abbott Emerson Smith, who wrote in *Colonist in Bondage: White Servitude and Convict Labor in America, 1607-1776,* that one-half to two-thirds of all white immigrants in the American colonies after the 1630s came as indentured servants. I suspect that the white servant, ashamed to admit that his progenitors had been brought to these shores in almost the same fashion as the blacks, was more likely to tell his grandchild that his fathers landed at Plymouth Rock.

But I submit that the redneck was captive from the very beginning, that his mind and bones and sinews were steeped in the "politics" of those who brought him over to the New World, and that he was responsive for a long time thereafter to the stratagems and philosophies of those who shaped the Southern culture in which he continued to breed. He has pinned his hopes and visions on many stars — from Robert E. Lee to Huey Long, from General Nathan Bedford Forrest to General Douglas MacArthur, Franklin Delano Roosevelt and George Wallace, and most recently, from Bert Lance and the Reverend Jerry Falwell to the Reverend Pat Robertson. But he has never been a full partner in the dreams and causes of the region.

The South stands where she stands today, I think — neither integrated nor segregated, neither bused nor unbused, neither an integral part of the nation nor a nation unto herself — because the redneck has never been a party to any of the alliances formed or the truces written.

There have been many alliances. The first issued from the old paternalism, the noblesse oblige, which has now fallen into such disfavor as surely to be gone forever. But it was more than just paternalism. It was a working relationship between two groups, the aristocratic whites and the blacks. But it failed. The alleged religion of the South was Judeo-Christian, but the alliance between the upper-class white and the black failed because the ethics of the Southern aristocracy were not Judeo-Christian, but Greek and Roman; their politics were not democratic, but Stoic. By that is meant that among the Stoics ran the political conviction that sovereignty inheres *naturally* in the best man.

Novelist Walker Percy said it well in an essay on Southern Stoicism in *Commonweal* twenty-five years ago. He reminded us that if this notion of the right to rule was well-suited to the Empire of the First Century, it was remarkably suited to the agrarian South of the last century. And he also reminded us of William Faulkner's character Colonel Sartoris, who made himself responsible for his helpless freedmen, and of Lucas Beauchamp, who accepted this leadership and formed a tight alliance with the Colonel. The upper-class whites allied with the freed blacks, Percy insisted, "not because [the blacks] were made in the image of God and were therefore lovable in themselves, but because to do them an injustice would be to defile the inner fortress which was oneself." It was the Stoic notion of creation's hierarchy whereby those at the top behaved justly, decently and gentlemanly toward those they ruled at the bottom.

The black Uncle Tom served as diplomat and messenger between his people and the white gentry, and between these two groups a sort of truce was drawn that lasted for more than half a century. There was peace, caused, I believe, by the fact that a large segment of society was not a factor in the truce — that is, the lower-class white masses, the rednecks.

The blacks were partners, albeit subservient ones, in the alliance because they were still useful to the gentry. But the poor white was not even needed, and thus there was no Stoic obligation toward him.

So the white masses got restless. They stood in their cabin doors and watched as Colonel Sartoris passed out necessities of life to the blacks: a house to live in, food, medicine, churches, a piece of land to farm, money to make the year's crop and help when he got in trouble.

The restless rednecks could have been a problem, because the poor whites had what women and blacks lacked the right or ability to exercise after Reconstruction. The poor whites had the vote. The blacks, with their right to vote suppressed, did not need to be feared. But because the redneck could vote, he posed a threat to the alliance between the Colonel and Uncle Lucas. The Colonel and his class, however, were in charge of politics in the South, and they were masters of psychology. They found in the two groups who could not vote — women and blacks — a specter to haunt the poor white men and make them compliant.

It was easy, over liquors and cigars after dinner or at the plantation commissary or crossroads store, to devise a strategy by which the voting redneck could be convinced that if he insisted on the egalitarian activities of the Populist movement or the farmers' alliances, blacks would grow restless in their unequalness too, that the suppressed energies of the black males would be unleashed, and they would rebel and find their mark, their prey, in white womanhood. In the wives and daughters of the redneck. For the redneck, for the sake of his women, the security of the system lay in his supporting it with his votes, and it was the Colonel's system.

It was the Colonel's religion, too, that shaped — or misshaped — the redneck and contributed to his peculiar view of the world — although not at first.

The Reverend Will D. Campbell, a well-known prophet, poet and proclaimer of a message of reconciliation rarely heard in conventional pulpits, at ease on his Tennessee farm.

Nothing has been so grossly exaggerated as the religiosity of the nineteeth-century rural South. It simply did not exist. The climb to identity with the institutionalizing of *that* religion began and largely ended during the latter years of that century and the early decades of the twentieth. Later, the brush arbors gave way to white frame Baptist and Methodist buildings at virtually every crossroad, and steeples began to emerge in every town, announcing to the world that redneck religion was on the way.

But that was later. The strong and established religion that existed before the Civil War belonged to an aristocracy steepled with the spires of Calvin and Henry VIII. So the blacks who were "converted" received their instruction in the faith out of a sophisticated brand of orthodoxy. The poor white's religion, however, was not the educated and well-tutored Stoicism of the aristocracy; it was a vague, varying and ill-defined folk religion, a combination of old wives tales, Indian lore, and half-remembered biblical passages passed around between visits from the circuit riding Methodist or Baptist preachers who came through on their way from Philadelphia to Natchez.

It was not until the system of slavery was threatened that the Colonel's church reached out to embrace the redneck. By and large, as James Silver's *Confederate Morale and Church Propaganda* makes clear, it was "Christian" leadership that provided the morale to justify secession and to sustain the Civil War. "God had entrusted to the Southern people an organized system of slave labor for the benefit of the world and a blessing to themselves while imparting civil, social and religious blessings to their slaves," the Reverend Thomas Smythe of Charleston wrote. "God now spake as with a voice from Heaven saying, 'Come out of the Union, my people.'"

Preacher after preacher spread the gospel of the South across the region to all its people, and almost unanimously, they identified Abraham Lincoln with the king of Egypt and Jefferson Davis as another Moses, leading his people to certain triumph. "God is in the war," the Reverend Henry Tucker, professor of belles-lettres at Mercer University proclaimed, addressing the Georgia Legislature. "He brought it upon us."

Perhaps never before had there been so much evangelizing in the midst of battle. And it is this fact, I believe, that accounts for the rapid increase in church membership during the Jim Crow era. That is what led to the development of an institutionalized religiosity not present in the region until *after* the Civil War was over.

But it was a tragic thing that the institutional religion of the redneck was developed as a call to arms, because a surviving redneck might have fought desperately for the slave society of Dixie in the front lines at Chickamauga, yet when the war was lost, he was left destitute and alone. And used. He had no one to help him with his physical needs, no one to help him with his psychological needs. So he turned to hating. And it was a religious hate. His hate was now centered in a redneck religion that had been founded on violence. During the war, for the first time since indentured servanthood, the redneck had been crucially needed by the aristocracy. Regiments had to be raised, and the church had been vigorous and effective in convincing the redneck that he was part of the system, one of God's chosen people.

The aristocracy put its mark on the redneck and then, exhausted by the war, left it to burn in him. His religiosity, his alienation, his need to depend upon himself bred a resentful and fervent, a suspicious and determined and independent class of people in the South. And as the years passed and they moved into trade and into town, a passage in William Faulkner's *The Town* described them.

"Ours [is] a town established and decreed by people neither Catholics nor Protestants nor even atheists but incorrigible nonconformists. Nonconformists, not just to everybody else, but to each other in mutual accord. A nonconformism defended and preserved by descendants whose ancestors ... quitted home and security for a wilderness ... to find freedom in which to be incorrigible and unreconstructable Baptists and Methodists, [and] not to escape from tyranny ... but to *establish one.*"

Thereafter, the redneck would span the breadth of Dixie with one of the most powerful religious machines ever known in the history of Christianity. Hundreds of denominations and sects would be founded, then split with each division becoming even larger than the original. He would take the antics of the aristocracy — card playing, dancing, drinking whiskey, fiddling and messing around on Saturday night — and make of them cardinal sins.

As well, the redneck would become the most patriotic of all Americans, fighting her wars, defending her most reactionary political values and institutions, shunning the new, clinging to everything old. He would become the champion of *The Faith* and *The Nation,* for he would virtually equate the two. But he would stand off from the mainstream of society with a suspicion bordering on open hostility.

And all of this would be an honest and basic faith. It would be a true commitment. For example, the redneck response to the "God-Is-Dead" theology would be two hundred fifty thousand bumper stickers, printed and distributed by the United Klans of America and found on thousands of pickup trucks around the South, saying: "My God is not dead, sorry about yours," and signed, "UKA."

Then — in contrast to the fact that the redneck servant had been driven *to* the land by the deceptions of the rich — thousands, and then millions of poor whites were driven *off* the land by those who came to *help.* Dressed in the sheep's clothing of TVA, AAA and other New Deal agricultural programs that were soon appropriated by the gentry and almost as soon exploited to the point that the end result was the current curse of agribusiness (again, with no place for the redneck), twentieth-century *helpers* have driven the redneck off the land.

But this time, without the hoe to lean on, he gazed on

alien ground.

In Pittsburgh and Gary, Chicago, Detroit and Dayton, the redneck would find himself stranded, and he would again harbor suspicions of the mainstream societies he encountered among Yankee Baptists and Methodists. And in time, his children would move to Berkeley and Denver, Houston, Dallas and Los Angeles. But this time, unlike in earlier eras, the redneck had packed his nonconformist religion for these journeys, so he would desert the denominational names in the North and would join the overnight sects. Satellites with a Southern axis would seek him out and succor him with the same strange mixture of other-world hope and nationalistic imperatives — the two together being to them the Kingdom of God. Meanwhile, his children would subscribe to the cults of the sixties, and to the New Age philosophies that followed.

I believe the point can be made that the *original* redneck was not the Southern farmer leaning against the hoe, nor the French peasant or painter or poet. From a religious standpoint, the original redneck surfaced within the sects and cults among Old Testament Judaism.

Perhaps no book ever written is filled with more potential anti-Semitic material than the Old Testament, because it is an honest book, written by and about themselves. Perhaps the Assyrians were just as bad, but it isn't expressed. It doesn't come through. The very people who wrote the books were the elect, the "called of God," yet make themselves out to be true rednecks — contentious, forever murmuring, grumbling, hating, never satisfied. And in their acts of worship, it often came through.

Especially was it true of some of their cults and sects, what might be called the Pentecostals of Israel. The Recabites, for example, described in Jeremiah 35: real standoffs, have nothing to do with anything new; don't drink wine; don't build houses, plant fields and vineyards. And the mainstream of their society saw them as the rednecks they were. Yet they really did *believe* something, and they were faithful to it.

In both the redneck of Israel and the redneck of Dixie, there was adequate historical reason for their discontent. They believed something enough to hate and kill about.

Recall that the religious expression of our redneck, historically, was mingled with piety and with hate. The same is true of a large segment of Old Testament Judaism. Consider the 137th Psalm and the fall of Jerusalem to Babylon, which the Psalmist was lamenting: "If I forget you, Oh Jerusalem, let my right hand wither away.... Remember, Oh Lord, against the people of Edom, the day of Jerusalem's fall when they said, 'Down with it, down to its very foundation.' Oh Babylon, Babylon, the destroyer. Happy is the man who repays you for all you did to us. Happy is he who shall seize your children and dash them against the rocks."

Then compare these ancient words to a Klan rally. Hear the mournful sound of "The Old Rugged Cross" sung by ten thousand voices. Watch the faithful march around the thirty-foot cross and hurl their personal, lighted torches at the base, soaked with gasoline and diesel fuel until it is lapping its tongues of fire to the black sky. And imagine: "If I forget you, Oh Atlanta, Vicksburg, Oxford, Donelson.... Remember, Oh Lord, against the Yankees, the night they drove old Dixie down! When Sherman said, 'Raze it, raze it, burn it down to the ground!' Happy shall be he who takes your little Yankee babies and slams them against Stone Mountain."

Redneck religion, then, is one force which ensures that he will not, once again, be left stranded as Markham has described, "... stolid and stunned,/ A brother to the ox." Not unlike the cults and sects of Old Testament Judaism — the Pentecostals or rednecks of Israel — the modern redneck is preparing for the messiah. And why not? It was through the ancient likes of them, the most unlikely of all, that God brought forth the Christ.

The redneck messiahs.

What then shall we say of our redneck brothers and sisters? Again, I hope that you do not judge this a simple glorification or romanticizing of either the redneck or the Klan. What I am trying to say is that the alleged redneck is a crucial factor to the social problem of race/poverty/war. I am trying to say that the redneck, too, while being manipulated, used and abused, has clung to individualism. And from this dogged determination there may yet emerge deliverance for that body from the ghastly specter of race and poverty that stalks and haunts and infects our land.

How, then, "will it be with kingdom and with kings," Markham's poem asks, "With those who shaped him to the thing he is,/ When this dumb terror shall rise to judge the world?" In the campaign of 1988, the redneck was judging and he was judged. He will judge for the nation in November. But as one who sprang from the loins of this nation's rednecks, I am wary, because I am familiar with the judgmental terms:

For with what judgment ye judge, ye shall be judged;
and with what measure ye mete,
it shall be measured to you again. ■

III.

Truth and Power of the Myth

Elizabeth Fox-Genovese

A distinguished scholar of wide interests, Elizabeth Fox-Genovese has served since 1986 as director of Women's Studies at Emory University, in the city culture that was the home of that fictional ideal of white Southern womanhood, Scarlett O'Hara. Writing extensively on both black and white women in Southern history at various junctures of her career, Professor Fox-Genovese had used Miss O'Hara's character as the point of departure for an article on "The Southern Lady as New Woman" in 1981. In Within the Plantation Household: Black and White Women of the Old South, *to be published by the University of North Carolina Press this fall, she works to unravel antebellum myths, while exploring the importance of race and class in the experience of women of that era. A 1963 graduate of Bryn Mawr College with a doctorate from Harvard, Professor Fox-Genovese has written or co-written scholarly books on topics ranging from economic and social revolution in eighteenth-century France to the relationship between slavery and the expansion of capitalism. Works in progress include a collection of essays on feminist theory, politics and culture and a study of the changing role of women in the Western world during the transition to capitalism. With her husband, the noted authority on slavery, Eugene D. Genovese, she is also at work on a book called* The Mind of the Master Class, *which will focus on antebellum planters of the South.*　■

107

The Real, Short Life
Of a Southern Lady

**F**or many, the image of the "Southern Lady"
is one shaped for eternity by the picture
drawn of the antebellum South in Gone
With the Wind. *It depicted a romantic
world of balls and hunts and chivalrous
men, in which white slave-owning women were treated as
noble ladies were when Europe was ruled by kings. It was —
or seemed to be — a world of pampered women, of absolute
white privilege, utterly supported by black servants who
bathed the children, planted the fields and washed and
ironed and cooked and sewed grand dresses for a planter's
ball. But the reality was something quite different, as we see
in the life of Sarah Ann Haynsworth Gayle. She was the wife
of a governor of Alabama, a slave owner, a woman of some
means and a beauty grown old and wasted — toothless — by
the time she was thirty. She was dead at thirty-four. This is
her story, one more typical of the times than Scarlett
O'Hara's.*

Sarah Ann Haynsworth married John Gayle when
she was still a girl — by her own admission a wild
one — not quite sixteen. Her journal and letters of-
fer glimpses of what the twenty-eight-year-old man
must have seen in her — and of the life, times and identity
of a slaveholding woman in frontier Alabama during the first
third of the nineteenth century.

Sarah Gayle was not the most polished, cultured, or even

pious of slaveholding women, but she was gifted with a genuine literary talent and a distinctive charm. Were her story written as a novel, the interlocking of themes would appear to defy real life.

Her fragmented and discontinuous journal, which captures her everyday life and thoughts, reflects narrative choices as surely as any fiction. But the choices that endow her narrative with such coherence were not entirely hers to make. For if her choices reflect the self-conscious and unconscious workings of the mind of a special woman, they also testify to the conditions of life in Southern slave society that lay beyond her choice. Those conditions also governed the lives of innumerable other slaveholding women, who expressed their personalities more discreetly but who, like Sarah Gayle, worked with the materials that lay to hand.

The Gayles came from slaveholding families and firmly identified with the attitudes and values of their class, but like so many others did not live as planters. Early in their marriage, they sold some of the slaves they had inherited and by the early 1830s probably owned only ten to fifteen.

During the years of the journal, Sarah Gayle divided her time between Greensboro and Tuscaloosa, Alabama; at its close, she was preparing to move to the coastal city of Mobile. During those years, John Gayle practiced law, served as a judge and embarked on the political career that would earn him a seat in the state Legislature, the governorship, and, eventually, a seat in the United States House of Representatives. Just as John Gayle's career typified those of other transplanted South Carolinians who were playing such an important role in Alabama, so did hers.

The adult life that Sarah Gayle depicts in her journal consisted primarily of the normal round of childbearing and rearing, household responsibilities, supervision of servants, worries about money, visits to friends, concerns with religion and fears of death. As she wrote John in July of 1832, he would find in her letter:

"All news of a publick [sic] nature, and as for that which

belongs peculiarly to me, you know when there is the usual health, that one day is but the double of the other — a chance visit, the going to Church, shopping, an odd volume read, an odd page written — and when the long list of seams and hems and gatherings added, my life is given, at least the mode of spending it."

Traces of the impetuous girl linger in the woman who importunately concludes a letter to her husband: "oysters! oysters! oysters!" but her intermittent journal for the late 1820s and early 1830s shows her maturing.

When only twenty-four, she notes that the marks of time on her friends' faces tell her that the "gay lovely, sparkling creature" she knew herself to have been she now "would scarcely know." The enchanting girl has given way to one who is "large, roughened, almost toothless, smoking and chewing! — the scolding manager of the family of four children."

Near her thirtieth birthday, she notes that she who had married as a child now looks older than her husband. "A woman, no matter how much younger she looks, at her marriage, soon fades except in rare instances."

What she can so plainly recognize, her husband cannot fail to see, she writes. "Good Heavens, what a sight I shall be in a little time! I will not write sentimentally, or I would tell you, charge you, beseech you, to let the affection, my pride and joy, and all upon earth endure even after this wreck of all that belonged to youth."

Sarah Gayle invested her deepest yearnings for love, unquestioning acceptance and connection in her husband. She also recognized the difficulties of holding a husband's interest and affection.

In 1828, she noted with unaccustomed anxiety that, for the first time in their married life, "Mr. G. stayed from me 'till long past midnight." The circumstance was too novel to permit complacency, or even sleep. She did not blame him, could not be so disingenuous nor such a fool "as not to know unless home is lit up by chearfulness [sic] and good humor, it will lose its attraction to the kindest and best — that he has always been that to me my inmost heart freely acknowledges."

But she cannot refrain from contrasting her need of him with his engagement in a larger world. Knowing that in marriage, as in the world, the relations between men and women remain unequal, she worries that her domestic concerns will bore him.

She ruefully acknowledges "my own perplexing quarulesness [sic] — my want of command over my temper — the carelessness with which I betray whatever gives me either uneasiness or displeasure." Add to that, she allows her naturally plain face to "express the utmost sourness, and whatever else is disagreeable dare I murmur that this forbidding countenance should be left for something more pleasing?"

These fears invariably resurfaced as the anniversary of their wedding approached, especially when John Gayle was away from home for the day itself, as he often was. In December 1827, she wrote of it to him, with a prescience that their lives would confirm:

"Do not let the 12th of this month pass by, without giving a smile and a sigh to 'auld lang syne.' It was our wedding day, and they are talismanic words, to wake up all that is precious and hallowed in memory. Dear, dear period — if I had been asked to single out from the whole earth, a being exempt from care, and in possession of perfect happiness, I would have laid my hand on my own bounding heart, and said, 'She is here.' And am I not yet? There is but one only drawback, a single shadow, the path before me, and that is that it must end — that it may be in a few years, perhaps months, the survivor will ask the question, 'Have I ever been happy?'"

Normally, she preferred to have Mr. Gayle at her side during her moments of pain and danger, even at the risk of giving way. She especially dreaded the unavoidable circumstances that took him from home near the time of her confinements. In 1829, toward the end of a pregnancy, she con-

In her office, Elizabeth Fox-Genovese sits amid a spread of papers, materials and books about the Old South.

templated the possibility that he would be away when she delivered. She allowed that it was trying for a man "to witness the sufferings of his wife then, but I own I am too selfish not to covet the comfort and support of his presence during the trial."

Sarah Gayle's feelings for her daughters and sons shed a special light on her sense of herself. On one terrifying occasion, as related in a journal written for her daughters, a horse ran away with her oldest son, Matt, and she could do nothing to control it. Matt called to her as the horse dashed past.

"... And if he had been kill'd happiness would not have visited my heart again. I love my daughters very dearly do I love them, and all that is amiable & good, intelligent & lovely would I have them, but all I possess of ambition, pride & the hope that steps over the threshold of home all such is centered in him, and if Death had crushed them, I should have mourned as Rachel."

Sarah Gayle deeply accepted the social attitudes of her class and region. If, during her husband's protracted absences, she frequently coped with complex household activities, including the management of occasionally difficult servants, she invariably insisted upon her need for his presence as master: "Oh! Come home, for mercy's sake, what *can* a woman do without her husband?" And, for all her generosity and warmth, she mercilessly dismissed those whom her social position did not oblige her to know. "Nothing renders a personal acquaintance necessary between us," she wrote pointedly about a newcomer to the neighborhood.

Living in Alabama in the 1820s and 1830s, Sarah Gayle took slavery for granted. It provided the underlying condition of her life and pervaded her sense of herself in the world. As the context of her life and identity, slavery brought out her best and her worst and her everyday in between.

She did not find the supervision of slaves easy, especially

when John was away from home. Once, like so many other slaveholding women, she gave vent to her deepest impatience with that unending responsibility, allowing that she despised herself "for suffering my temper to rise at the provocations offered by the servants. I would be willing to spend the rest of my life at the north, where I never should see the face of another Negro." But that was a bad moment, and she did not otherwise oppose slavery, which she knew to be the foundation of her society.

The quality of Sarah Gayle's life depended heavily on the labor of servants. The time she spent reading and playing with her children or visiting her friends depended upon their performing all of her basic housework and helping her with child care. When she mentions household tasks in her journal, she refers to "having" them done or to supervising their being done. And despite her boundless love for her children, she consigned most of their everyday supervision to servants.

She did regularly complain about what she saw as her servants' laziness and impertinence: "I believe my servants are going to craze me." Yet she also shouldered her own responsibilities for what she perceived as her servants' ungovernability, allowing that "indulgence has ruined them — they are idle yet full of complaints." She had no confidence that her orders were being obeyed and even obedience "is accompanied by murmuring, sour looks & often surly language, that almost put me beside myself. . . ."

When, after repeated trials with a particular servant, Hampton, she threatened to sell him, Hampton treated the threat with contempt and "said he could not be worsted, and was willing to go."

For all her troubles, Sarah Gayle formed deep attachments to particular servants. Throughout the late twenties and thirties, she wrote in her journal and to her husband of her longing to repurchase Mike and his family, whom they had earlier sold.

Never before had she pushed Mr. Gayle in this way, nor

would she now, "but that it does seem to me I cannot be happy unless it is done." By her account, Mike shared her desire to be reunited.

During the years in which she did not own Mike, she knew where he was, who owned him and the names and ages of his children as they came along. She would not likely have been better informed about distant relatives or friends. Yet it never crossed her mind that this family should be free.

She saw nothing contradictory in the expression of her deep affection for — and emotional dependence on — people she proposed to hold in perpetual slavery while fully acknowledging their ability to take care of themselves and her.

Rose, a servant whose death left Sarah Gayle without a nurse, had come from her father's family. "She was raised at my feet, and was my child's nurse, a most kind and excellent nurse, and the play fellow of all my children." Rose died in April 1834 of lockjaw, which she had contracted from a large splinter in her foot.

Rose lay ill for three weeks "during all which time, I thank God, I did not leave her day or night." Sarah Gayle closed Rose's eyes and "in tears and fervor prayed that God would cause us to meet in happiness in another world." At that moment, she knew "that color made no difference, but that her life would have been as precious, if I could have saved it, as if she had been white as snow."

The entire family attended her burial. Thereafter, the children's countenances would sadden "when something occurs to remind them of poor Rose, and my own heart will swell as Haynsworth [her son] sings snatches of the songs his nurse taught him."

Sarah Gayle's text shows Rose's life intertwined with that of her white family but offers no clue about Rose's own kin or attitudes. Possibly she, like Sarah Gayle, had intermingled black and white families beyond easy disentangling. If Sarah Gayle grasped the equality of souls before God, she accepted the inequity of ranks in this world. Within households, personal ties crossed class lines. Slaveholders and slaves participated in a shared imaginative universe that could shimmer with mutual affection or, as in the case of Hampton, shatter in mutual antagonism.

For her warmth, compassion, humor, intelligence and love for her family, black and white, Sarah Gayle ranks among the most attractive women diarists of the early nineteenth century. But her finest qualities cannot be divorced from her willing complicity in a social system that permitted itself to flourish through the enslavement of others — cannot be divorced from the inequities that she accepted and perpetuated. Her experience and perceptions as a woman depended upon the social system in which she lived. Her ineffable charm cannot be severed from its social moorings.

Religion figured centrally in Sarah Gayle's sense of herself, as it did for so many other American women. She lived intimately with the fear of death — for herself as well as for those whom she held most dear. Sickness, epidemics, childbirth, the dentist — all evoked the "Angel of Death." The fear of death flickers through her journal, never reaching fever pitch, never paralyzing her, but always ready to flare up.

Religion provided the most promising antidote, the most satisfying consolation against loss. But for Sarah Gayle, the struggle for faith remained precisely a struggle. She never joined a church. As she told Mr. Gayle when they were discussing which church to attend, she cared nothing about one denomination or another, but "would give worlds to possess that faith which triumphed over the fear of death, and looked with hope and confidence beyond the grave."

Sarah Gayle had been preparing for her own possible death at least since she began bearing children. During the early 1830s, when her health was poor and her spirits occasionally low, she returned to the prospect. In 1831, she actually sat down and drew up instructions for Mr. Gayle to follow in the event of her death.

He must, she insisted, do as she proposed: "No stepmother for my poor girls — she may be an Angel for you, but very different for them." She was right to concern herself with the fate of her girls should something befall her.

Because of the limitations of his craft, the dentist loomed large in Sarah Gayle's story and its ending. He inescapably confirmed her awareness of her rapid aging. And, in his futile attempts to arrest the decay, he inflicted a pain that surpassed bearing.

When she was twenty-four, her teeth especially worried her. "This loss of my teeth has been the severest mortification to which my vanity has ever been subjected." She grieves at their loss because she shrinks from "the idea of appearing to so much disadvantage in the eyes of that one for whose dear sake I would still, if possible, preserve some trace of youth."

In July 1835, when Mr. Gayle was away from home, she braved an operation on her teeth. Had she foreseen its horror, she would never have consented. "The torment of filling the tooth is unspeakable." Yet she was glad that Mr. Gayle was "from hence — my little courage always leaves me when he is hear [sic], for I really feel as if his presence could lessen the pain, or do away the necessity of enduring it."

The dentist proved her nemesis, Rose her precursor. Sarah Gayle, like Rose, contracted tetanus. Servant and mistress, equal in vulnerability before the deadly disease, were unequal only in the means of contracting it. Sarah Gayle would not have picked up a splinter in the yard: She would not have gone unshod. Rose would not have had complications from dental work: She would not have gone to the dentist — a doctor who occasionally puttered with teeth, maybe; a town dentist, not likely.

When Sarah Gayle fell ill, John Gayle was away in Indian territory trying to restore their fortunes by speculation in Indian lands. As she had so often feared at the moment of her confinements, he did not hear of her illness in time to see her alive. That absence was hard to bear, although the absence of the man whose love and care permitted her to give way to her fears may have helped her to face the death she had so dreaded with the courage she would have wanted.

Just before dying, she mustered her strength to pen a final message: "I testify with my dying breath that since first I laid my young heart upon his manly bosom I have known only love and happiness."

John Gayle returned the love, writing: "My wife is the great engrossing object of my affections. In comfort she is indispensable to my peace, and a consciousness of her love is essential to my existence."

Sarah Gayle's daughters did get a stepmother. ■

Sarah Gayle's journals and letters are located in the Bayne and Gayle Family Papers in the Southern Historical Collection at the University of North Carolina at Chapel Hill, and in the Gayle and Gorgas Family Papers in the Hoole Special Collections at the University of Alabama at Tuscaloosa. Complete documentation is provided in Dr. Fox-Genovese's forthcoming book, Within the Plantation Household: Black and White Women of the Old South *from which this account of Sarah Gayle is drawn.*

Pat Conroy

Wavering between desires to be a great author like his hero, Thomas Wolfe, or a great Marine aviator, to rival his father, on whom the book, The Great Santini, *was based, Pat Conroy appeared to tip the balance in 1963: He enrolled at that all-male bastion of the South's chivalric tradition, The Citadel. But in one of life's ironies, Conroy emerged four years later not as a military man but as a writer. Today, he stands as one of the most original voices in the literature of the South, a region he claimed as his own — tortured soul and all — after a childhood spent bouncing around its small towns as a military brat. After writing* The Boo, *a memoir about a favorite teacher at The Citadel, which he published at his own expense in 1970, Conroy launched his professional writing career in earnest in 1972 with* The Water Is Wide, *an account of his experiences as a maverick teacher on South Carolina's Daufuskie Island. Four years later came* The Great Santini, *the first in a trilogy of novels — including* The Lords of Discipline *and* The Prince of Tides *— about growing up in a region where confrontations with issues of family, religion and patriotism were unavoidable. Since 1972, Conroy has lived primarily in Atlanta. "The South is an obsessive theme with me," he has said. And within that theme, as part of it, is another: the enormous and continuing influence of his mother, for Pat Conroy was raised to be a Southern man.* ∎

Mama and Me: The Making of A Southern Son

My mother made no real distinction in being Southern and her belief in life after death. There was a seamlessness to her life and she appeared to be a woman of absolutes. She thought that being Southern was a state of unearned grace and proof of a loving God in the universe. I think she found it peculiar that God would even bother to create the rest of the world. She was the prime source of the myth that she lived and died with her sense of place as steadfast as it was unexamined. Peg Conroy spent her life being underestimated by people in the morning and studying their heads that afternoon. My mother was always at her most charming the night before she cut you up for bait.

No Southern man will ever understand himself until he learns how the South cripples its women, and I have studied the pools and depths of my mother's own damage in the system for years. There were a thousand faces to both her delights and sorrows and dozens of imperiled masks in the calendar of moveable feasts she designed in her constant version of herself. Though she knew there was a conspiracy in the South to make its women stupid, she was also aware that the women themselves were the major enforcers of those codes of air and smoke. Because of this, my mother never presented a single Southern woman for your inspection, but came at you in sets, cotillions and swarms. The only thing that remained the same was her Southernness. It was the single constant in her diffuse character, and I never was sure if it contained either the elements of hazard or salvation for her. The South had marked her so well that I'm not sure I ever knew which mother she submitted for my inspection was actually mine. A coalition of pretty women, all claiming my mother's face, raised me along the Atlantic seaboard to be a Southern man.

When my mother remarried after an honorable and ultimately dispiriting career as an officer's wife, she began to invent a history of her family that did not exist. Her ancestors became aristocrats of the highest order. Her family was many things, but aristocratic it had not been for many a long millennium. She began to add the clean lines of Georgian manors to tar-paper shacks in Alabama and placed my grandmother's modest Virginia-Highland home on the National Register and the Dogwood Festival Tour of Homes. When my mother reconstructed our history this way, I thought it was a deceitful yet pixilated form of lying. But she reminded me that when I did the same thing every day of my life, I congratulated myself and called it the art form of fiction.

My mother was trying to make my stepfather, Dr. John Egan, believe that he had married into high cotton indeed. She spoke of pristine manor houses astir with the murmur of well-trained slaves from Senegal and the singing of happy field hands bent over the greening fragrant acreage of money crops. Alex Haley and his book *Roots* had inspired my mother to research her own family's distinguished, unpraised history, and she had discovered that "we descend from the most aristocratic and largest slave-owning family in Alabama." My mother confided this with such abundant pleasure and my stepfather sighed with such gratitude that he had married into such unimpeachable stock that I felt somewhat cheap when I asked her what had become of those peerless forebears. The only thing my mother had not discovered in the golden realms of our lineage was that we had actually owned Kunta Kinte, and I wanted to discourage the full range of her myth-making.

"The Depression," my mother whispered. "They lost it all in the Depression. Every last acre."

Dr. Egan nodded in sympathy and understanding as I writhed in complete discomfort. He did not understand that my mother's re-creation of her familial sources had little to do with genealogy, but everything to do with the fact that she had read *Gone With the Wind* when she was a thirteen-year-old Atlanta girl and the book had christened her in all the unquenchable fires of Southern romance and revisionist history.

"Your father's people, of course, were pure trash," my mother said.

My mother read *Gone With the Wind* aloud to me as a child, and it remained her favorite novel until the day she died. She claimed to have read it over thirty times during her fierce career of self-improvement as a reader, and she had stood among the inner-lit crowds of Peachtree Street when the movie premiered in Atlanta in 1939. She lost count of the number of times she saw the movie, and I lost count of the number of times she took me to see it when I was a child. It was the first long book she ever read aloud to me, and the novel is as much a part of my growing up in the South as the sight of sunlight on the flanks of the Confederate horsemen riding in perpetuity on the side of Stone Mountain. By the time I was in high school, I had read the book four times and my mother and I would spend long hours discussing our favorite scenes and characters in the book. I learned much about the extraordinary powers of fiction by my early study of Margaret Mitchell and those long talks with my word-struck mother. She was imprisoned by the book's magisterial aura and authority, and I watched my mother transform her sometimes unhappy life into rites and ceremonies of transfiguration by making the book part of both our lives. There was always a religious component to her devotion to the book. It was not land my mother and her family had lost during the Depression, but all the imagery of their distinction and all the signs of their luck and self-worth in the Southern scheme of things.

My pretty mother had been hurt because she had been born poor. I never knew a woman who lusted so openly for gentility, for the grace and prestige of a family history she would never have. During her whole life, she burned to be what she could never be. So *Gone With the Wind* became the King James Version of her own reclamation and remaking of herself in the image of Scarlett O'Hara. In the forties, Scarlett O'Hara was the colorist and sculptress who united the hues and shapes of a certain garden variety of Southern woman who came to ripeness under her imprint. Because of her, it is still one of the strangenesses of Southern life that our women are far more interesting than our men, yet spend their entire lives trying to hide and deny that fact.

I believe my mother unconsciously spent all her days pretending she *was* Scarlett O'Hara, that somewhere nearby a camera was rolling and invaders were crossing into the homeland and my mother's city was ready to burn and the wounded were beginning to scream in the railyard. She always had the sensibility of an unemployed actress. When she met my lean and flight-jacketed father outside Davison's department store, I believe she confused him with the gallant, civilized appearance of Rhett Butler. Never has a first impression proved so erroneous. My mother, in all the comeliness of her social innocence, could not recognize the primitive howling of Chicago in my father's hellbent approach to life. The only thing my father shared with Rhett Butler was a uniform and a testosterone level. By mixing both metaphor and geography, my mother brought the memory of coarse streets and the discriminations of Studs Lonigan into the history she was composing for all of us.

When my mother married a Conroy, whose family originated in the Irish county of Roscommon, she thought she was being true to the spirit of her one heroine. O'Hara. She remembered the O'Hara name and that Scarlett was Irish, wildly, proudly, demonstrably Irish. She aligned her fate to a

Atlanta novelist Pat Conroy understands the Southern experience. His best-selling trilogy, The Great Santini, The Lords of Discipline *and* The Prince of Tides *conveys his knowledge of a region he says: " . . . is an obsessive theme with me."*

warrior's code and a man who would kill far more enemy soldiers as a night fighter and close-support bomber than Rhett Butler ever saw when he rode for the Confederacy. It took me years to recognize the great leap my mother took when she accepted my father's proposal and agreed to spend the rest of her days as an officer's wife. My mother invented herself as she went along. I never saw the cunning strategies she employed in the subtle craft of her mothering as she began to turn me into a Southern male with her seal of approval stamped along the high margins of the packaging. Nor did I notice the distinctive moment my mother began the long, curious process of turning me into a Southern writer who would tell my mother's own story to the world.

My mother held a great and closely guarded secret: She thought she was every bit as fascinating as Scarlett O'Hara. I also held a secret close to my chest. I agreed with her completely. Though I rose to manhood in mean kingdoms in the country of Southern white men whose sensibilities were unrefined and rough around the edges, my mother spent her life sharpening my eye for absurdity and detail.

She raised me in the knowledge that the world of platitude is the native tongue of the white Southerner. She would lead me into Southern homes and have me count the books I didn't see and point out the number of Southern homes with more guns than books or more duck prints than ideas. Southerners have a perilous attraction to safety, and nothing is revered longer or held more sacred in the South than a bad idea. The South fell in love with creeds and entitlements set in concrete and left the thinking to other parts of the world. My mother saw this as the great strength of the South and what she both loved and hated about it the most.

To her, the brilliance of Southerners had always been in the vanity of their recalcitrance, their limitless ability to say no, to hunker down in red clay among the signal fires of the brotherhood, to retreat into the fortress of their own stubbornness when knowledge and all its fresh armies arrived bristling and immense at the city gates. She even knew that

Southern women led the war against themselves. There is no outcast condemned to solitude like the Southern woman who refuses to conform to the crippled lockstep of the sorority, and my mother felt like an initiate with this insider's information. The Southern woman was the only human being she could name in the Western world who could come close to raising a majority to vote against her own equal rights. A woman of the South always deferred to the menfolk, at least until the children were grown. That is why the South shines with brilliant, ebullient grandmothers and why my mother waited over thirty years to divorce my father. She left him the day after his retirement from the Marine Corps, the first terrifying day without a uniform that he faced the world not as a warrior, but as a man.

I t was history, then politics, that first divided my mother and me. In college, it began when I first started to question the greatness of *Gone With the Wind*. Now I see it as intellectual bullying in the college boy armed with a dozen courses in literature taking on the defensive woman who never spent a day enrolled in college — but then I saw it as an act of great courage and a chance to educate the woman who had taught me everything she knew in the world. It was cruelty that made me say that her favorite book was a pale Southern version of *War and Peace* with some of Tolstoy's passion and none of his genius. Margaret Mitchell, I said, was an apologist for the unspeakable stupidity of Southern white men. She was the chronicler of those Southerners who prove over and over again that democracy can support the very worst instincts of a free people, and because of her book the South would always maintain its charming nostalgia for evil. I told my mother that Margaret Mitchell had written a great book and that it did not contain a single word of truth. What I didn't know and didn't say is that her son did not have a single grain of humility at his disposal. I was despoiling the text of her liberation.

It was during the middle of the civil rights movement,

and History had traveled South for a second time and had come to seek the white boy out in all the privilege and fatuous helms of his rigidity. Because I was raised to be a Southern boy, I knew there were two tribes and only two tribes in the South, and I learned how to be an Afrikaner long before I learned the braver creed of being an American. I could put my hand to my white breast and feel the cold drumming of the South African's heart. Black men and women began to act out the literature of our times in the street. It took a people in bondage to remind Southerners how precious freedom was, and how a life was not worth living without it. People who could not vote taught Southerners the most indestructible civics lessons. No Confederate riders ever taught the world as much about the highest precincts of Southern honor as the black marchers who led us through the bloody-throated nightmare of those times. No book had ever come close.

Because my mother taught me how to read, she taught me also how to feel. She thought I blamed all that was wrong with the South on *Gone With the Wind.* She was wrong. I blamed it all on her. I could not make her see the South as I saw it. Through reading, I began to make elaborate associations that I found irrefutable and she found ridiculous. When I read about the death of Anne Frank in Bergen-Belsen after completing the diary whose humanity left *Gone With the Wind* in dust and blood and shame, I asked my mother why the words of Anne Frank did not change the world enough to let Martin Luther King Jr. use the men's room in the Dinkler Hotel in Atlanta. If she had survived, I continued, Anne Frank's husband could not have joined the Piedmont Driving Club. I asked her why the scent that defines our century was not by Revlon or Max Factor, but the lingering odor of Zyklon B high among the tiles of gas chambers in Poland. Self-righteousness was my theme, the one interior note I struck with astonishing regularity. But *The Diary of Anne Frank* was another gift of my mother, and she had taught me early on that reading was a dangerous activity and could change the way you lived your life. Even as we fought, she savored the triumph of her one unsubduable vision. Though she could not write books, she looked upon the raising of her children as the fruit of her quiet genius. We saw the world through the prism of her singularity. Though we were Southern, she had cut us loose from the herd.

In 1984, after writing four of the books that made my mother both furious and proud, I came to the room where she would die of leukemia. There is no book on Earth, no literature so powerful, no words so stricken to prepare a son for the death of his mother. I came to that room as a Southern man, and I almost strangled on the words of love that lay unspoken in all the soft places of my throat and tongue. Again, it was imagination that failed me as I tried, in absolute silence, to tell my mother the infinite ways I loved her and owed her and was grateful to her for the life she had opened up for me. She was fifty-nine years old and still as pretty as a girl.

In the last month I told her that I heard a rumor that the heirs of Margaret Mitchell were looking for a novelist to write a sequel to *Gone With the Wind.* She thought it was a terrible idea and was glad she wasn't going to be around to read it. Yet the idea intrigued her and we began to discuss scenes that the sequel could contain. An affair with Ashley Wilkes and the birth of Prissy's first child with Scarlett in kind attendance. She also thought that Rhett Butler must die at the end of the book and that the scene of Rhett and Scarlett saying goodbye should be one of the greatest in American literature.

My mother asked me how I would write the sequel. I told her I couldn't write the sequel because *Gone With the Wind* was too interconnected with my love for her and the serious business of being her son. Instead of one sequel, I would authorize five or ten if I were one of the Mitchell heirs. I would love to see the South through the eyes of John Updike or Norman Mailer or Joyce Carol Oates or Saul Bellow where I could learn things about Scarlett O'Hara never imagined in a Southern sitting room. Or I would have selected black writers like Alice Walker or Toni Morrison or Ishmael Reed to write a sequel that would burn like a brand in the consciousness of our times. In the landscape of literature there are a thousand Scarletts and Rhetts waiting to be born in the portable hermitage of the writer's imagination. All the characters waited for rebirth, I said, lying suspended and unanimated in the pure world of possibility, waiting for ignition into life.

"No," she said disagreeing. "Those writers you named would just Yankee it up."

I brought books to her bedside, far more than she would ever have time to read. Often, she would read them all night long as I slept on a cot in her room. The chemotherapy began to kill her long before the cancer did. She would vomit through the night, and the diarrhea humiliated her before nurses and children and strangers. Slowly she lost her hair and I shopped for wigs in a half-dozen Atlanta stores before I found ones suitable to replace my mother's lovely hair. I thought I could look at her death as a writer would, but kept tripping over my invisible identity as her son. The toll of the leukemia was fierce. In slow degrees it began to relieve my mother of her extraordinary beauty. It began to dismember the substructures of her appearance.

I have not told you enough about my mother's beauty. When she took me to see the movie *Gone With the Wind* I could feel the pleasure of the audience at the uncommon chemistry created by Clark Gable and Vivien Leigh. But I would sit and watch the film with the amazing knowledge that I was sitting with a woman who read stories to me each night and who was prettier than Scarlett O'Hara. My mother's prettiness delighted her and everyone around her. By stealing that gift, the cancer began the process of making my mother want to die.

On one of those last nights my mother could not sleep, and I woke to see moonlight on her undermined cheekbones and tears running down her face. There was a smell of vomit and excrement in the room. Her wig had fallen off her head and lay on the floor beside her bed. She weighed eighty pounds and the prettiest girl ever to turn the heads of boys from Druid Hills would be dead within the month. I hurt all over trying to think of the perfect words to say to my mother.

She spoke first.

"Are you writing about me in your new book?" she asked.

"No, Mama," I answered, "I'm not."

"You're lying," my mother said. "I can always tell when my children are lying."

"You might not like what I'm writing about you," I said.

"I'd like you to promise me one thing," she asked.

I went to her bedside and said, "You're in a great position to bargain, Mama."

She turned toward me, turned the blue eyes toward me that not even the cancer would touch and said, "Don't write about me like this. Make me beautiful."

Oh, Mama, I said that night, oh mother of mine, I'll make you so beautiful. Because you made me a writer and presented me with the gift of tongues and a passion for language, I can lift you off that bed, banish the cancer from your cells forever, restore your shimmering hair and your lovely figure and set you singing and dancing along the margins of my books forever. When they speak of beauty in the South, my mother, they'll invoke your name and praise the immense high passions of the men who desired you and the children who were never a match for you.

It was the last promise I made to my mother. It was the same promise she made to me when she began to read to me as a child — when she opened up the universe with all the magic canticles of the language.

When she went into a coma, my sister and I read her poetry from morning till night. I tried to read her the first chapter of *Gone With the Wind*, but could never get past the opening page. I wanted to send my mother out of the world on a great wave of the English language. I thanked my mother with poetry on the night she died in my sister's arms, on the night I made my last covenant with beauty and the responsibility of being Southern. ■

After a childhood spent bouncing around small towns in the South as a military brat, Conroy today stands as one of the most original voices in the literature of the South.

IV.

The Importance of Place

Anne Rivers Siddons

Anne Rivers Siddons came of age as a writer just as Atlanta, the natural capital of a region finally forced from Old South to New, was coming of age as a city. A keen observer of the city's development, Mrs. Siddons grew up as the daughter of a lawyer in Fairburn, a nearby small town that is now a suburb. At Auburn University, where she majored in art, she was features editor of the college newspaper. Returning to Georgia after her 1958 graduation, Mrs. Siddons attended the Atlanta College of Art and worked in advertising before joining the now celebrated stable of writers assembled at Atlanta *magazine by editor Jim Townsend and managing editor Bill Diehl. Her first book,* John Chancellor Always Makes Me Cry, *was a collection of essays published in 1975. It was followed the next year by a highly regarded novel,* Heartbreak Hotel, *about an Auburn undergraduate coming to terms with the civil rights movement. She followed with* The House Next Door *and* Fox's Earth, *and her 1987 novel,* Homeplace, *was met by raves. In the book, a native of an Atlanta suburb similar to Fairburn returns home after years in New York and finds herself caring again about things she thought no longer mattered. Her latest novel,* Peachtree Road, *describes the transition of Atlanta from big town of the forties to yuppie-driven metropolis of the eighties.* ∎

137

The Maturing of a City:
Atlanta Comes of Age

ack there, in that dreaming cradle slung between Camelot and catastrophe, there was in Atlanta a golden decade known as the sixties, and a small group of men called The Club, who minted the gold.

It was the best of times, period. There wasn't any worst. Oh, there was a shadowy underside, perhaps, a deep-running current of black water at the hidden roots of that exuberant, sunstruck time. Of course there was. This was the South in the middle of the twentieth century; this was a small, truculent Deep South city only just beginning to struggle up out of stasis. How could there not be shadows on the grass in Eden?

But during that head-spinning, heart-leaping decade, it was easy to overlook them. Or, if we noticed, it was not difficult to excuse, even approve them. So touched with magic was that Midas-fingered group of men who rethought the city, and so glittering was the new Atlanta they raised, that even the plagues and puzzlements of that time had, for a benighted span of years, a kind of impetuous glamour, a slapdash, headlong sorcery. They were the mirror images of progress, begotten of outreach and growth — and growth, after all, was the Grail. For ten years at midcentury, Atlanta was more properly Atlantis, a city brushed with fire and grace, and it was a spectacularly wonderful town in which to be young.

That was the key to Atlanta in the sixties, I think. It was such a *young* town. Young in years ... none of the slow, seductive blood that ran in the blue veins of the exotic coastal cities such as Charleston and Savannah and New Orleans silted the trumming peasant veins of Atlanta.

Young in ethos ... the small group of men who piloted us out of the somnolent Deep South and into the thin, crackling blue air of the Sunbelt were themselves at midprime going into that decade, at the very peak of their powers. In their day, they were as potent as wild stallions and as full of vitality.

And young in the ways of the world ... at the dawn of that ball-bearing decade, the world at large seemed far away from Atlanta. Change was roiling deep below the placid surface, but it was unseen and unremarked. Up top, on the sun-dreaming surface, we seemed as motionless and eternal as some sleep-drugged, beautiful little Brigadoon. And we were about as canny and sophisticated as its terrible, time-frozen and utterly charming denizens.

Oh, yes. No matter what it was before or what it became after, Atlanta at the beginning of its great trajectory was a splendid town to be young in. I was in my mid-twenties then and in love with the life and times of my newly adopted city, and would have loved anywhere I found myself. But it seemed to me that everyone around me was young, too, and everywhere I looked, the sheen and gloss and high, leaping blood of youth glimmered and dazzled. Youth bloomed in the soft city nights like green April; youth burned from the downtown skies like white August; youth sat warm on faces and forearms like the high honey sun of October. It was as if Atlanta woke up from a hundred-year sleep and found itself, not old like Rip, but fiercely and joyously and ass-over-teakettle young.

I thought at one time that the sixties began, in spirit if not in fact, when the CBS cameras panned from Richard Nixon's blue-Buick jowls to John Kennedy's all-enabling white grin during the first historic television debate on September 26, 1960. It was the first glimpse we got as a nation of the essential flame at the heart of Camelot.

But now I think that for Atlanta, and for me personally, the sixties began when I drove past the electric sign in front of the Darlington Apartments on Peachtree Road on my way home from work and noticed that our municipal population was more than a million. I still remember the little "frisson" of sheer pride and delight that danced up my spine at the sight of those sparkling digits. A million. A million people, eccentric and particular and kicking, living in this city that was now my city, too. And it *was* a city, by God; nobody could argue with all those numbers. Take that, New York and Chicago and Los Angeles. Take that, Birmingham and Charlotte and Tallahassee. I could hear, now, with new equanimity that oft-repeated, mean-spirited little chant of the outlander: "If Atlanta could suck as hard as she can blow, she'd be a seaport."

Seaport or not, we were a city of a million people, and no bush-league Atlanta basher could change that.

After that, the sign in front of the Darlington became as the green light at the end of Daisy's dock to Gatsby: talisman and totem and pure panacea. A city. We were a real city. Figures never lie.

Coming out of the fifties, as the city swung sluggishly into the orbit of Camelot, we had need of talisman and panacea. We whistled in the dark even as we swaggered in our seersucker and dressmaker suits. For even if we did not acknowledge it, the average Atlantan could hardly fail to see what that group of men who remade us saw: that Atlanta was a city nearly asleep.

The majority of us closed our eyes and quoted those mesmerizing electric numbers to ourselves. But those men, fewer always than three dozen, stirred, blinked and became The Club.

At the close of the sixties it would be easier to see them for what they were and became: Old Atlanta, or what passed for it. Men with names like Mills B. Lane, Ivan Allen, Robert

Woodruff and Richard Rich, who had lived all their lives in Buckhead within a four-mile radius of each other, grown up together, gone to the University of Georgia or Georgia Tech together, flirted and danced with and married each other's sisters and cousins, godparented each other's children, laughed and wept and partied with each other, loved and sometimes hated each other, and often buried and mourned each other. Rich, or what the world calls rich, a good many of them; men who had built family businesses into international concerns; men who had made millions from Coca-Cola, either directly or indirectly; men who had dramatically altered the face of the South and in some cases the nation with their monolithic urban and suburban developments; men who had, almost singlehandedly or in concert with five or six of their peers, in the firestorm decade of their ascendance, brought the city a major league sports arena, five professional sports teams, a great white arts center and a world-famous conductor to inhabit it, a world-class international airport, a state-of-the-art rapid transit system, a freeway system to boggle the mind, unparalleled convention facilities and the guests to fill them, and the harmoniously integrated school system that lured in the industry to fuel it all.

But in the late fifties, on the threshold of the Great Decade, they were not yet The Club, and the city lay waiting for its kiss as Snow White did for her wandering prince's. The analogy is not as silly as it sounds. If Atlanta had and has an aristocracy — a doubtful proposition in a city so raw and new — they were its heirs and scions.

I have a friend, himself young in those days, who went on to found one of the South's first pure research institutes, who holds that Atlanta's future was assured when those young men returned from war. Those years were, he says, like a held breath, the preliminary gathering of muscle for the great leap of growth and progress. The young men who would guide the progress and shape its direction were not themselves fully aware of their inherent power and looming roles. They simply came home to tend to business and raise families, expand fortunes and build lives. But when they looked outward, the world according to Atlanta shifted on its axis.

Since their births, they had known each other and moved as easily in one another's homes and clubs as they did in their own. It was always that proximity, that mutual pool of kinship, that gave them their unique force and focus. Its basis was the psychological similarity of class attitudes that made them so effortlessly comfortable together. They perceived and acted almost as one. Their concerted social antennae were awesome.

I have always thought that the secret of their extraordinary power was that proximity and an unusual sense of mission, their unquestioning acceptance of the mantle of leadership that fell onto their shoulders. It is not a unique phenomenon; it has happened before, this fortuitous marriage of money, civil, social and political power. It happened with the Greek city-states, with the Medicis and to a limited extent with the church in the Middle Ages.

There was another factor in their singular success story. The Club was smart, if never wise, about the matter of race. Wisdom would have walked a further measure, seen a longer way down the road. But it *was* smart, and for that incendiary decade, it sufficed.

But when these men paused and looked around, they can't have liked what met their eyes — a city stagnant since the flurry of building directly after World War II, crying out for office space and air facilities to catch the faltering torch the railroads had dropped. The last tall building in the city's gap-toothed skyline had gone up almost a decade before. Atlanta had always been a service city, a mover of goods, a branch office town, but now business and money turned away in impatience, going elsewhere, because the wheels at home were not numerous or sturdy enough to take the weight. They saw business after business come south, sniff around, find little to their liking in the way of facilities and quality of life and head for New Jersey or Texas. And they saw a formless black population, large and growing, with as yet no real muscle, but with an enormous potential for it.

They were not stupid men, nor shortsighted; they knew, even if they espoused it personally, that segregation could not and would not prevail and that when it crumbled, they could either profit from its fall or be crushed beneath it — but fall it would. Being consummate businessmen, they began to put their feelers out to the black community. Far better to have the Negroes of Atlanta buying from their businesses than burning them. Far better to lure Northern business south with the promise of open, peaceful schools than put their burgeoning strength behind a last romantic schoolhouse-door stand that was doomed to failure before the first federal marshal appeared on the scene.

They were well-connected men, even in those early days; they knew what the tenor of the nation's highest courts was and that bullheaded defiance of a federal ruling on school integration would tip Atlanta back into the quagmire from which it was painfully struggling. Mayor William B. Hartsfield had the right idea but the wrong syntax: Atlanta was not so much a city too busy to hate as that in Atlanta, organized official hate was bad for business. Those twenty or twenty-five men put aside their plates at the Capital City and Piedmont Driving clubs and began to reel in the lines all of them had into the blasted streets and projects of South Atlanta. And they began to talk.

And so the marches came, and the sit-ins, and the boycotts, and The Club talked. And when the integration ruling came down, they instigated the Sibley Commission to study the school situation and see what could be done. And it served to get a dialogue going, and it kept the school doors open and the Northern money rolling south. And the jailings and shoutings in the heights and the running in the streets continued along with the talking, and Mayor Ivan Allen

Mrs. Siddons recalls the air of excitement as a new day dawned with roaring optimism in the Atlanta of the early sixties.

stood atop a car during an incipient riot in the black Summerhill neighborhood before he was toppled, talking, talking; and the news out of Birmingham and Selma and Little Rock and Oxford came smoking in over the wires, and every blinding summer day dawned on another threatened riot in one embattled black Atlanta community after another. But The Club talked, and Atlanta did not burn. In the end, the men of The Club talked, and the black leaders listened, and white Atlanta, reluctantly, opened most of its doors.

It wasn't, despite what the Chamber of Commerce did and does tell anyone who will listen, a particularly exemplary handling of race; often it was not even decent handling. The motives behind it were never pure. They were, simply, business. The business of Atlanta has always been business. In Atlanta, if it is good for business, it is as good as done. Most of the action came at least ten years too late. But it came, and it came without clubs and dogs and fire hoses and blood and death in the streets of the city. I think it came because the men who would soon be The Club had their ears open in the late fifties.

And they were willing to talk until hell froze over.

They were an impressive group, sitting together at one of their luncheons or board meetings. Attractive, easygoing, affable, with their own rough, ritualized jargon, the argot of the well-born Atlanta man among his peers. "Hey, how you doin'?" one seersuckered man would say to another, smiling a slow smile and laying an arm easily over a shoulder. "Hey, good to see you, suh!" That drawled *suh* was the group's familiar, as *tu* is to the French. It was not used outside the ranks.

But the ease and indolence were by way of protective coloration. To sit at lunch in the Capital City Club or the Commerce Club was to see pure power in repose, drinking its ritual pre-lunch bourbon and branch water and eating its London broil. It was almost palpable; you could get dizzy from it.

In the end, the way they did it all was with money. There

was enough money at home to do what needed to be done —
to accomplish what was set out in Ivan Allen's Six Point Pro-
gram for revitalization announced at the beginning of his
term in 1962 and to accomplish The Club's own unspoken
but equally far-reaching agenda: to keep the good life in
Buckhead good. Enough to light a decade into flame and
dazzle. Enough to fire the rocket and send Atlanta soaring to
the very edge of the known universe. After that, the money
would have to come from somewhere else, and they knew it.
They knew even as they started out, even as they mapped its
course, that theirs would be a self-limiting journey, that they
themselves, as a political entity, would be doomed by their
own success.

I remember sitting one night after work in the lounge of
the Commerce Club, drinking old-fashioneds with Jim Town-
send, the supercharged new editor of *Atlanta* magazine, who
had just hired me at half my former salary to come and work
twice my former hours. Around us were several of the men
on the rise and the make who would soon be The Club; they
were listening, as everyone listened, to Townsend. I sat qui-
etly, stricken silent with awe at actually being in this all-
male Holy of Holies and in the company of so much raw vi-
tality and power. It is, in my head, Ivan Allen who said it,
but it well might have been someone else; Ivan Allen shone
over those days like a young sun and was the spokesman for
a decade and a generation. And so it is his face in my mind,
and his voice, but at any rate, someone said, "We can do it at
home. We have enough money here. We have *just* enough.
After that, it'll have to come from outside, and God knows
who and what will bring it in. But for now, we have enough
and we can do it."

I have never forgotten that night and those words. Do it?
Lord, did they not do it! A major league sports stadium and
teams to fill it? We can do that at home. No need to go bor-
rowing outside. A rapid transit system, a new freeway sys-
tem, a new airport? Let us make a few calls. We can work
something out. Direct flights to the capitals of Europe, of-

fices and consuls of many major countries in the world on Peachtree Street? New skyscrapers and branch offices of nearly every Fortune 500 company, office parks stretching for hundreds of square miles in the five counties around us, shopping centers in every community in the same radius, apartments and hotels and restaurants and shops and housing . . . give us a year or two.

We can do it ourselves.

I really don't know why they came together to reshape Atlanta when they did. I think perhaps they just happened to grow up together in a relatively quiet period, when nothing else really occupied them and they could stand together looking out. Maybe it's just that simple. They were never really a complex group. Their very simplicity was one of their great strengths. I think I know, though, what ended their regime. It was two things, really.

One was that the city they launched simply didn't stop. It exploded. It became, in that one decade, a city too big to be perceived all at one time. For a group with a single great unified and focused vision, that was the first mortal blow.

The second was that they never really took the blacks seriously enough. It is difficult to understand why they did not see that one day, all that fragmented voting power would come together at the polls, all that force and restlessness would find one voice, or at least a voice strong enough to demand the political reins. But I don't think they did. I don't think that most of them thought that that was where the political muscle would lie, once the outside money came to town. And it is a private theory that it was hard for them, by that time, to conceive of power and largeness that was not bestowed by them, but taken. Several of them were quoted, in interviews given during the sixties, as saying that, of course, in Atlanta the Negroes would always be consulted, but . . . . And an eloquent shrug would be shrugged, and a half-smile smiled.

All the young, gold-dipped Achilles have heels of lead where the gods have held them. The Club's was blindness to the potential political power of the blacks. Toward the end of the sixties, the oars went over to the galley slaves and to the newcomers and the new money in town, and The Club came down off Olympus and out of City Hall and went back to Buckhead. For the most part, they handled that transition as well as the one that preceded it. With the exception of an embittered few, I think they were probably glad to see, as the Irish say, the back of that singular time. By then, the payoffs must have seemed few and far between.

In a way, for me and for the city, the sixties ended with the assassination of Martin Luther King Jr. After that, the center could not and did not hold, and the sixties turned into another place entirely, a place of beads and fringe and hard rock and pot and LSD and the smoke from burning bras and bridges and neon-colored death in green jungles that nobody could name, in a war that nobody understood and few wanted. Atlanta's eyes were forced to turn at last from itself out into the world, and perhaps to our own surprise, we found it good. Or at least, absorbing. After that, there was no turning back inside.

But while it lasted — in the headlong, heart-spinning, gold-bitten, high-bouncing decade that it rode like Hippolyta — there was no place on Earth like Atlanta. Excitement ran in the streets like spilled mercury; music and exuberance and high spirits and portent and promise poured into town on a flood of restaurants and clubs and theme parks and theaters and galleries and high-rises and shops and sports and fat, flashing egos and seemingly endless money — and all the world was young.

I remember one night in early April, toward the end of that time, when a group of us from *Atlanta* magazine whirled directly from work to the opening of a new cocktail lounge to the opening night of a new play at a new theater to late supper at a new restaurant and from there, finally, to listen to Ramsey Lewis at Paschal's La Carrousel. And then, in the green-smelling, moth-winged hours just before dawn, we ended up wading in the dark, cool water of a little lily pond in Ansley Park.

"I'd like to catch this night by the tail like a comet and hold it, so it would never end," somebody, probably me, said.

It was the early morning of April 4, 1968, and in only a few hours, the man whose Nobel acceptance speech we had all attended with bursting hearts would be dead in Memphis. And with it, the decade we had thought was our own would die, too.

But for that moment, just for that one breath-held young moment, in a young city riding a comet's tail, it was three a.m. on a moonlit morning in spring, and all things seemed possible. ■

Eliot Wigginton

Though he grew up in Athens, Georgia, as the son of a University of Georgia faculty member, Eliot Wigginton was never happier than when roaming in the remote reaches of the North Georgia mountains. After earning a bachelor's degree and then a master's degree at Cornell University and a second master's degree at Johns Hopkins, it was to those mountains in Rabun County that Wigginton returned to become a high school teacher. There, he has developed innovative teaching techniques that are at once progressive and conservative, conservative in the sense that they help students learn a deep respect for the richness of their region's traditions, even as those traditions are evolving. Georgia's Teacher of the Year in 1986, Wigginton has become an authentic voice of the Southern Appalachians, and with his students, who have produced the nine-volume Foxfire *book series as well as the* Foxfire *magazine, he has brought an appreciation of that culture to a wide national audience. Wigginton founded the Foxfire Fund, a non-profit educational corporation, in 1968 and serves as its director. The editor of a dozen books and author of numerous magazine articles, he wrote a book for public school teachers,* Sometimes a Shining Moment, *that won the 1985 Kappa Delta Pi award as the year's best book on education and the 1986 W.D. Weatherford Award for outstanding writing about Appalachia.* ∎

The Mountains: A Different Mix of Politics

*I*n 1977, Aunt Arie Carpenter, then nearly ninety, still cooked on a wood cookstove. She lived alone on the side of a mountain in Macon County, North Carolina, in a log home with no indoor plumbing and no heat save that from her fireplace. Sometimes, on winter nights, when the wind outside was blowing snow, my high school students from adjacent Rabun County, Georgia, in their Nike running shoes and prewashed jeans, would pull up close to the fire with her to shell and "parch" popcorn from her garden in a tin "capper" wired precariously to the end of a broomstick.

Memories of those nights are indelible, permanent. And the stories. A favorite was about the time their hunting dog woke Arie and her husband, Ulysses, one night yelping at a possum he had treed. They hauled themselves out of bed, dressed and went outdoors where Ulysses, nearly blind, pointed his rifle in the general direction of the racket, Arie got up close behind and aimed it for him, and he pulled the trigger and brought the possum down.

Another concerned voting. One of Arie's great frustrations was over the fact that every time she and Ulysses went to vote in a national election (and they never missed an opportunity), he'd make her go into the polling place first. When she was finished, he'd follow, cast his ballot for the opposition and "cancel" her vote. Every time. Until finally, shortly before he died, she outsmarted him, voted second and canceled his.

Sometimes it's like that in the mountains.

Our piece of the Southern Appalachian region — North Georgia and bordering counties in East Tennessee and western North Carolina — was "made safe" for white immigrants relatively late in the history of this country. The first settlers came in the late 1700s, and they lived in relative peace with — sometimes even marrying — the Indians who were there first. But it was not until 1837 that President Andrew Jackson, who was born in these mountains, ordered the remaining Cherokees rounded up into stockades, held like cattle and then herded on foot to a new reservation created for them in Oklahoma. The casual connections between that action, the discovery of gold in Dahlonega, Georgia (America's first gold rush) and the establishment of a federal mint there in 1838 are all historically clear, but that's another story. Immigrants flowed in primarily from England, Ireland, Scotland and Germany, homesteading on formerly Cherokee Indian land, in tracts of two hundred fifty and four hundred ninety acres, acquired by lottery at a cost of less than twenty dollars per tract.

Some brought, or soon acquired, slaves — a fact that confounds a widely held belief that mountain people were never slaveowners. True, there weren't many. There was so little bottom land for farming here that slavery was never an entrenched economic necessity as in the Deep South. But there were some. I have in my classroom at Rabun County High School a copy of a will, dated 1849, in the hand of John Kelly, patriarch of Rabun County's Kelly family, that reads in part:

"To my daughter   Lucy Derrick [I also leave] three negroes   Ned a man about thirty-five years old Lizabeth a girl about fifteen years old and Washington a boy about sixteen years old also all my household and kitchen furniture and farming tools....

The negroes given to the said Lucy Derrick ... together with the increase of the negro girl Lizabeth are at the death

*of the said Lucy to be sold and the proceeds thereof to be
equally divided between my Grandchildren."*

According to Andrew Ritchie, who wrote the sole history
of Rabun County to date, there were two hundred forty-eight
slaves here in 1862 owned by sixty families.

The majority, however, owned no slaves. The angry de-
bates preceding the Civil War, therefore, propelled the resi-
dents of most mountain counties into the dilemma of their
lives. Complicating the dilemma was the fact that, rather
than slavery itself being the central point of difference, for
many it was instead the issue of Secession. When the Geor-
gia Legislature met in Milledgeville in 1860, after the elec-
tion of Abraham Lincoln, to decide whether to take the state
out of the Union, one hundred sixty voted for Secession and
one hundred thirty voted against it. The two Rabun County
delegates, Samuel Beck and Horace Cannon, both of whom
owned slaves, voted, like all the other representatives from
the North Georgia counties, to remain in the Union, avoid
war and fight for States Rights (including the right to own
slaves as guaranteed by the existing Constitution) "within
the system."

With Secession came war and, for many mountain resi-
dents, the continuation of what had become a terrible con-
flict: to fight for the North and attempt to preserve the Un-
ion, or to fight for a United States of the South. Whole
families split over the question. In his autobiography, North
Carolina state Superior Court Judge Felix E. Alley — who
was born in 1873 in Aunt Arie's North Carolina county —
writes about his father, Colonel John H. Alley, who believed
the North had absolutely no right to dictate to the South
how it should manage its internal affairs and thus fought
with the South. And he also writes about his uncle, who hon-
estly believed North Carolina had no right to secede and
thus fought with the Union — along with, according to Alley,
some two hundred thousand other mountain men.

Most counties in North Georgia contributed men to both
sides of the conflict. The percentages varied, from a nearby

county where it is said the Union flag flew from the courthouse dome throughout the war, to our county where far more men fought for the South than for the North. Whatever the percentages, the more germane point is that the conflict had a dramatic impact on the political cast of Georgia's mountain families, many of which, for years after the war, remained unflinchingly Republican in a state that was almost entirely Democratic.

There were exceptions, of course. After the war, Judge Alley's father never mentioned the event again to his brother, Alley's uncle, who, "different from most Southerners who served in the Union Army, lived and died a Democrat, and for thirty-six years cast the only Democratic vote that was cast in Pea Ridge township."

But for whole families, a voting pattern was set that remained — in some cases still remains — in place and unshakeable for decades. Mountain politicians came to know on whom they could rely for support. Georgia's Lieutenant Governor Zell Miller, a Democrat from adjacent Towns County, wrote in his book, *The Mountains Within Me*:

Last names immediately tell one the party to which a [Towns County] person belongs. All Taylors are Democrats; all the Shooks, Republicans. Likewise the Brysons, Dentons and Plotts are Democrats, and the Corns, Garretts and Woods are Republicans.

Of course, there have been notable exceptions, the best example being the Collinses of Union County. The present Commissioner is Ned Collins, a Democrat, who defeated Republican Gene Collins by a few votes, who had been elected by one vote over Wayne Collins, a Democrat. ... The split in the Collins family occurred in the generation living during the War Between the States and Reconstruction.

There are parallels in Rabun County. The overwhelming majority of families here has been, and still is, Democratic. Republicans, in fact, are hard to find in this county among "natives." A friend of mine here, however, who has been embroiled in local political frays of his own, shared with me almost conspiratorially the names of two Rabun County families who have "always been Republicans — all of them."

That is not to say there is no movement, though, or that party loyalties are as rigid and inflexible as mountain granite, for the fact is that as Georgia began a long slow journey toward the Republican Party — spurred most recently by the waves of prosperity that have swept over Atlanta — the mountains became more heavily Democratic.

It is fascinating to watch these shifts and speculate on their origins. It is tempting, for example, to hypothesize — and here I must say that I am no historian, I have not researched this issue in any depth and I may be completely off base — that the Republicans lost some of their early support in the mountains during the period of Reconstruction when government troops in charge of the militia districts into which the mountain counties were placed began to enforce such burdens as a newly imposed federal tax on homemade whiskey. The extent to which the production of corn liquor was common practice is hinted at by a telling sentence in the same 1849 will cited earlier in which John Kelly orders that his hogs and cattle be "seized and two Rifle Guns and a buggy together with my still and tubs" and sold by his executor "as soon after my death as it can be done."

I can almost hear furious conversations following the war in which mountain families, perhaps grateful to Andrew Jackson (and the federal government) for securing land for them, and perhaps thus deciding to stick with the government twenty some years later in its time of need, suddenly perceive themselves as having been double-crossed.

And it is tempting to hypothesize that the Republicans lost still more of their remaining support during the Great Depression. Though mountain people, because many of them lived a basically self-sufficient existence on small farms and owned their own homes, were somewhat better equipped to withstand those years than their Atlanta neighbors, the fact still remains that until Franklin Roosevelt, there was virtually no cash in circulation at all here except for what little could be generated by hewing crossties for the railroad or by making and selling liquor illegally. The widespread perception in the mountains, therefore, is that Roosevelt saved America. In Rabun County alone, there were four active CCC camps and one large FERA program, the latter run by Frank Smith, the county ordinary, who, at ninety-two is still alive and well in Clayton, our county seat, and remembers those days with vivid clarity.

In a long interview conducted for *Foxfire* by some of my students, he talks about the fact that there was absolute poverty and hunger in the mountains in the winter of 1933, and when he opened the FERA office and looked out onto Savannah Street, he looked out into the faces of several hundred waiting men. A few of them were "too weak to stand up unless supported by holding onto a shovel. I would send them home with a grocery order and tell them to come back when they had regained some strength."

Years later, in the fifties, when I first began to visit the county, a framed portrait of Roosevelt still hung over the cash register of Gillespie's farmers' market in downtown Clayton, and it hung there until the store closed for good. And the legacy lives on.

Aunt Arie's *sole* means of financial support up to the last years of her life was her Social Security check (which, even in the late seventies, was less than fifty dollars a month). And one of the most serious crises I and my students faced came when we fixed up Kenny Runion's ramshackle home, and, because of its "increased equity" (a new tin roof and some Sheetrock), his tiny Social Security payments were stopped. We finally got them reinstated, but from that time forward grew accustomed to individuals to whom we offered similar help resisting, saying, "I'm afraid it'll hurt my check."

Buildings are still in use today in Rabun County that were erected by WPA labor and, according to Frank Smith, the county became so solidly Democratic that the only ones who opposed the New Deal programs were the few types

Wigginton has become an authentic voice of the Southern Appalachians. Working with his students, he has brought an appreciation of that culture to a national audience.

who had worked hard and created their own financial security and didn't have any patience with those who hadn't done the same. People, in other words, whose knee-jerk response to poverty then was (and still is?), "Those people just haven't tried hard enough."

Political cleavage along economic lines is so persistent in this country that it is no surprise to find that in 1988, rural Rabun County, with its low per capita income, remains overwhelmingly Democratic. It's no surprise to hear the older friend say: "Rabun County was all Democratic not too long ago. Even the ones who were Republicans weren't really Republicans. They were just against the Democrats. And most of the Republicans we have around here now aren't from here. They're all second-home types and transplants who have been brought in to run businesses and retired people with money that have moved in from away from here."

Like from Florida. Or from Atlanta.

And *there's* another interesting thread to unravel from the patchwork quilt of forces and perceptions that shape the political reality of the mountains: an inexorable population shift to a more equal balance of natives and outsiders.

People coming in from outside to look around is nothing new in the history of mountain counties. By 1882, the Tallulah Falls Railroad had reached our county line from the south and was bringing in summer tourists by the train load. They came to stay for weeks at a time in the twelve hotels — not one of which exists today — that were clustered around the spectacular Tallulah Gorge (after which Tallulah Bankhead was supposedly named following a visit there by her awed folks). By 1905, the railroad had pushed on into Clayton bringing tourism and tourist dollars into the heart of Rabun County — all this well before the state highway was paved in 1917. (In fact, our county still has over six hundred miles of unpaved public roads.)

Nor is the fact of people coming in to build summer cottages anything new in the history of the mountains. Just north of here, the Vanderbilts had their estate completed before the turn of the century. By the twenties, the Georgia Power Company. had its dams in place in Rabun County to generate hydroelectricity for its customers south of here, and the shores of Lake Rabun, one of the five resulting lakes, were dotted with the summer homes of wealthy Atlanta families.

But neither tourists nor summer people lived here year-round, and the demographic makeup of the county remained virtually unchanged.

Other forces were at work, however. By 1912, the U.S. Forest Service was well along on a five-dollar-per-acre purchasing spree that would eventually result in over sixty percent of our county's land being owned by the government. Georgia Power snapped up nearly another ten percent for itself. And when the day finally came that actually owning a second home in the mountains, or even moving there full time, became an attractive, viable option for many like myself (teachers, doctors, lawyers, owners of gift shops and motels and small businesses, retirees — all seeking to escape the urban alternative), the value of what little privately owned land was left skyrocketed. Local property taxes climbed, ratcheting upward along with the land's new value and to meet the increased demand for increasingly expensive municipal and educational services. As agriculture became less viable economically, some farms were sold to developers — or portions of them developed by their owners. Last year, there were nearly one hundred fifty individuals in this county alone buying and selling real estate as an occupation.

My high school classroom is Rabun County in microcosm. Students who were not born here are present in increasing numbers. Few of the students, both native and new, who go on to college ever return. Most who stay behind are native kids who go straight into agriculture or the local blue-collar labor pool (second home construction, the Burlington rug mill, businesses that increasingly provide services to tourists).

New families continue to arrive. Older families become decimated, fragmented and scattered. Change is in the air both here and in all the mountain counties.

And how will all this alter us politically? There are just too many forces at work to be able to predict. Certainly the shifts in demographics will result in a broader range of political opinions and alliances. Rabun will become less *predictably* Democratic.

But the blame for that will not come to rest entirely on the doorsteps of the Republican transplants. Sooner or later, the fact that the Democratic Party is becoming increasingly liberal must also take its toll here where the majority of mountain families are religious and deeply conservative — and where the young people who remain behind in those blue-collar jobs tend to take up that conservative banner and carry it on, sometimes in the form of a Rebel flag.

What that translates into in real life is a population that remains somewhat suspicious of the women's movement; is vocally anti-union, abortion, "secular humanism" and sex education; and profoundly anti-gay. Liquor stores are unique; "dry" counties are the general rule, and in those counties, like ours, that do allow sales of beer and wine, a restaurant or a convenience store that carries those products will lose its license for selling them after midnight or on a Sunday. A schoolteacher like myself can be fired for having a beer with dinner at a local restaurant.

That is *not* to say that mountain people are permanently bound by some ancient code of behavior. In the last several years, Betsy Fowler became the first woman ever elected to our local school board. Grace Watts made local history by being chosen mayor of Mountain City, Georgia, in a closely fought runoff election. Clayton got its first liquor store. And Rabun County High School got a family planning course. But the changes are gradual, carefully considered and frequently argued over to near exhaustion; and as the Democratic Party marches on ahead with its gay rights planks and its women's rights planks and its liberal pronouncements, some mountain people may drop out of the parade.

One final thread is worth a tug. In some ways, it is the most important of all, for it transcends all political loyalties at the same time it complicates them; die-hard Democratic voters will desert a Democratic candidate who fails to perceive it and runs afoul of its strictures. One cannot make sense of the mountains without understanding it: Throughout the history of this area, the most fervently angry and passionate reactions of mountain people have been reserved for those situations where other people tried to tell them what to do and in the process, sometimes unwittingly, butted heads with mountain value systems. In those situations where demands or proposals were made that were *perceived* by local residents as being absolutely unfair and unjust, nearly any negative reaction was — and still is — generally condoned as justified; it must be remembered that the oldest families here in the mountains are descended, for the most part, from people who immigrated in vigorous reaction against perceived injustice at home. "It" — this long thread — is a tradition with deep and honorable roots.

Examples abound from Civil War days to the present. It is not fiction, for example, that some mountain families, because of some obscure perceived injustice, have become embroiled in feuds that have lasted for generations. Neither is it fiction that revenue agents have been known to disappear forever. Shortly after he began to enforce the laws against the making of illegal liquor, county ordinary Frank Smith's wife was warned by a friend, "Don't let your husband go to this community. He might not come back."

Smith recalls, "I was fool enough to go out there to see if I *would* come back." He wasn't shot, but while he was there, he was confronted by one resident who was so furious that "he just trembled all over."

More recently, the outside world has wondered at periodic television news reports over the last few years showing the mountains shrouded in the smoke of scores of forest fires set by arsonists. Any Forest Service official can explain the basic outlines of the problem: During the years the Forest Service was purchasing mountainside land from local residents, there were no objections. It was the bottom land that was valuable, not the ridges and peaks. And though some general regulations and guidelines were subsequently put into effect regarding the harvesting of timber, the ranging of cattle and hunting, access to the mountains themselves was not restricted, and many of the regulations — those regarding hunting, for example — were not rigidly enforced. Stories of "hunting out of season" were common then, as they are now; and in many ways, the work of the Forest Service was seen as beneficial, for with the new service roads cut into the mountains to ease the work of loggers and firefighters, access to the woods was actually improved rather than impeded.

In the last ten years, however, there has been a not-so-subtle shift as the mountains have been "adopted" by the outside world and groups of environmentalists as a "precious natural resource" to be "preserved in untouched beauty for future generations." Mountain people have a healthy tolerance for those whose lifestyles differ from theirs — it is one of their most commendable traits — and the outsiders who moved in and formed bird-watching groups and mushroom hunting expeditions and anti-litter activities were widely regarded with good-natured humor by all.

But when their slow, steady pressure took the form of inventories of publicly held natural areas to which access should be limited and then pressure for legislation, it wasn't funny anymore. And when the Chattooga River, which forms the boundary between North Georgia and South Carolina and on which *Deliverance* was filmed, was declared a Wild and Scenic River and the Forest Service access roads were closed, some local people vented their anger and frustration in the only way they knew: They burned the woods.

I can't defend that action, but I can understand it. What one must realize is that it's *not* that local people don't want the mountains to remain clean and beautiful for their grandchildren; rather it is that they don't want the outside world stuffing unfair rules and regulations down their throats. Most of the land and the natural resources are held by absentee owners; the area industries are owned by corporations that have their headquarters elsewhere; much of the remaining economic activities such as home construction, the opening of gift shops and fast food restaurants and motels is dependent on non-local demand for survival. So, in an age when the outside world is seen as being already overwhelmingly in control, the desire to hang onto some scraps of "states rights" is palpable.

This year, the Mountain Protection Act sponsored by Zell Miller ran aground and cracked up on the same rocky shoals. A perfectly logical, commendable attempt to regulate mountainside development — and to protect Georgia's mountains from some of the same rampant abuse by greedy land speculators and developers evident in nearby Watauga and Avery counties in North Carolina — was perceived by local people as being unfairly restrictive. Rumors flew, with absolutely no justification, that, if the bill were passed, local people wouldn't even be able to cut firewood on their own private hillside land. And the controversy prompted a flood of letters to the editors of area newspapers. One of the more memorable surfaced in our own Clayton Tribune. Written by Woodrow Blalock, a local real estate salesman whose roots in this county go back for generations, it expressed the sentiments of hundreds in the lines, "I also believe we should preserve and protect our beautiful Georgia mountains but NEVER let the whole state have the power to control and tell us poor mountain people what we can use our little remaining private lands for."

One senses that some of the same emotions were at work last year in Forsyth County, where a sixties-style civil rights march was met by hostile crowds of local residents and attracted national media attention. Although some overt racism still exists in the mountains — as it does in Atlanta and Washington and Boston and Howard Beach, New York — mountain people tend to be far more tolerant than the national stereotype would have the outside world believe. Black high school students from Atlanta are regular visitors to my high school classroom, as are my students to those Atlanta classrooms; we have a black teacher-coach in our school who is tremendously popular and who is a graduate of our school. And I have worked with other teachers from Forsyth County who confirm that the root causes for the demonstrations that hit the evening news had less to do with racism than they had to do with a reaction against unfair pressure from strangers. Had the whole thing been handled differently, crowds might never have gathered.

The jury is still out on the degree to which any of this will affect political affiliations, but one guess can be ventured fairly safely: If outsiders are perceived as a force that brings along to the mountains an unwelcome agenda, and if they push that agenda in inappropriate and insensitive ways, there is no question but they will be met with hostility. (I'll never forget the story of the Florida man who came in, bought a large tract of land here, fenced it off and closed it to hunters, went out of town for a few days, and came back to find the carcasses of ten deer hanging by their necks from the rafters of his cabin's front porch.) And a parallel, but completely separate, result may be that if the majority of those outsiders are, in fact, Republicans, then local Democrats may become even more determinedly Democratic if for no other reason than that they've met some Republicans, and they haven't liked what they've seen. It's complicated, fascinating stuff.

The way to defuse all this, of course, is to have mountain people deeply involved in shaping the agenda from the start. Zoning is anathema in most mountain communities — another one of those outside impositions typically foisted on local residents by newcomers who have decided that the economic future of the mountains lies in tourism (and who decided that anyway? Ask many local residents, and they'll vote *not* for tourism, which is usually seasonal and always subject to the whims of a fickle public, but for stable, year-round employment in industries) and who have decided that tourists won't come to an area that isn't kept pretty and don't like their view marred by factories and auto body shops.

And since zoning is typically an outside agenda and an unfair imposition of will, it is routinely voted down, or, if put into effect, regularly subverted by local interests. Except in Helen, Georgia.

There, a dying mountain town was converted into a mock Swiss village that is one of the most popular tourist attractions in North Georgia and has one of the toughest zoning codes around. The difference? There, local people made the decisions. There, outsiders who wanted a piece of the action worked in collaboration with, not in spite of, local sentiment. And though there are some local people who don't like what Helen has become and who say they don't like the fact that all the town's economic eggs are in one seasonal basket and the fact that most of the businesses are owned by outsiders who provide only minimum-wage jobs for the local workforce, at least the town was saved. And everybody abides by the zoning codes.

I moved to the mountains in 1966. I was a Democrat then; I still am. I bought a piece of land on the side of Black Rock Mountain and, with the help of my students, built a log home that I still live in today. I had no desire for wealth then, still don't. I wanted to contribute something positive to the community, still do. I had the idea years ago that what mountain people needed to do was to close off the outside world, keep their kids at home to carry on the old traditions and preserve themselves and their culture intact like gnats in amber. Next, I listened. Then I grew up.

Change is in the air. I cannot advocate that my students stay at home and make lye soap for the benefit of spectators. I will not discourage them from attending college, even though it means they may never come home again. In fact, my Foxfire organization gives out twenty-five thousand dollars a year in college scholarships to Rabun County seniors.

And if the truth be told, I don't actually give a single damn if the mountains go Republican or Democratic or neuter.

But what I do care about is that the kids I teach, whether they leave or stay, have at least a deep-seated appreciation for all that was, and is, fine and honorable about the culture they represent. What I care about is the continuation, somehow, of a lifestyle where people still wave at each other as their cars pass in town and where residents still have benefit gospel sings for the neighbor whose house just burned.

What I care about is that the best of such traditions not get bludgeoned into oblivion by an outside world invading with its sights set on a piece of ground and a house as good investment possibilities, surrounded by a chain-link fence. And that mountain people, while retaining a healthy skepticism, suspend judgment and meet the outside world halfway with a hand stretched out in friendship, ready to cooperate until that world proves that cooperation is not what it had in mind.

When I think it's all impossible, as I often do, I try to remember Aunt Arie and the delight with which we greeted each other, outsiders and locals together, actually wanting nothing from each other but friendship.

I can still taste that popcorn. ■

V.

Black and Southern

Raymond Andrews

As the fourth of ten children growing up in a share-cropper's shack in Morgan County, Georgia, well before the Freedom Riders came on the scene, Raymond Andrews saw a South that a new generation of Southerners coming of age in more prosperous times never knew. His family was poor but its culture rich enough to launch both Andrews and a brother, the painter Benny Andrews, on careers in the arts. Though he's not just whistling "Dixie," Andrews shows that for him the old times there are not forgotten. They are fertile ground he continues to till in literature. At age fifteen, Andrews came to Atlanta to live at the Butler Street YMCA and completed night school at Booker T. Washington High while working odd jobs. Later, after leaving Georgia for the Air Force, he took courses at Michigan State University. But he was a thirty-two-year-old employee of KLM Airlines in New York when he launched his writing career with a story for Sports Illustrated *on the introduction of football into his community.* Appalachee Red, *his first of three novels set in fictional Muskhogean County, Georgia, won the first James Baldwin Prize for fiction in 1978. It was followed by* Rosiebelle Lee Wildcat Tennessee *in 1980 and* Baby Sweet's *in 1984. After years of living in New York and Switzerland, Andrews in 1984 came back South to Athens, Georgia, where he has completed two more yet-to-be-published novels.* ■

171

Black Boy and Man in The Small-Town South

*I*n the spring of 1867, Georgia's blacks organized a Republican Party and agreed to meet and unite with the state's white Republicans. That following July Fourth, at a state convention held in Atlanta, the merger occurred. Blacks became Republicans because this was Abraham Lincoln's party, the party of freedom. At the time of the Atlanta Convention, Georgia's House of Representatives had two members from Morgan County: Abram Dukes, a farm laborer, and Monday Floyd, a minister. Both were black. Both remained in office until 1872, when they received warnings from the Ku Klux Klan to return to the plow and the pulpit full time and forget all the politicking.

The Klan chased blacks out of Reconstruction politics but didn't take away their right to vote. That came later. Beginning in the 1890s, Georgia, like most of the South, became a one-party state and began instituting the "white primary" (which led to the poll tax), the "granddaddy clause" (if your granddaddy didn't vote, neither could you) and Jim Crow laws, making segregation of the races total. All of this was a ruse to disfranchise the black, a right the race didn't regain until 1946.

When I was growing up in Morgan County, four miles from the county seat of Madison, Georgia, during the Depression and World War II years, blacks weren't involved atall in the state's, or the nation's, voting processes. Despite the fact that many blacks closely followed the nation's politics, we didn't feel a part of that world. Elections meant nothing to us except to remind us we couldn't vote in them. We didn't feel a part of anything governmental except the Army ... and the war. We couldn't even vote for Franklin Delano Roosevelt, who, as far as Morgan County blacks were concerned, was America's first president since Lincoln. All the other presidents in between were just one faceless blur. Yet in state elections, we were needed and used. Needed not for our "non-votes," but for politicians to use us to scare the white voters. The master at this "niggerphobia" scare tactic was Georgia's Eugene Talmadge, the blacks' own "Lil' Hitler."

I can still remember the first time I heard him campaigning over the radio and saying something to the effect, "When riding about the state, I often see white folks out under the hot sun working in the fields and just on down the road apiece, I'll see niggers sitting on the porch in the shade. This, by golly, gotta stop!"

He must've gotten these folks out from under the hot sun up onto the shady porch and kept them there, because they sure kept voting him into office. That is, except for the term of 1943-47, when even God must've needed a break from such bigotry and gave us a four-year respite with Ellis Arnall, a man with more dignity. (Though nine-year-old me, at the time, had my doubts about Governor Arnall — this occurring when he took away the state's convicts' stripes and replaced them with a new, drab uniform. Having wanted to grow up to be a convict, just in order to don those out-of-sight stripes, I quickly lost all interest in pursuing a convict career once seeing these new dull, "Arnall" uniforms. I never told this to my parents, knowing old folks just didn't dig young folks' ideas on dress. Nor did my older brother Benny tell our parents that, during this same period, he wanted badly to be a hobo in order to travel.)

Talmadge won the gubernatorial election in 1946, but before taking office the beginning of that next year, he died. Before there could be any blacks dancing up and down the cotton rows, word went out that his son was inheriting the throne ... and the only difference between the two was the daddy called us "niggers," while the son called us "nigras."

But many black Georgians back then considered themselves fortunate. As the saying went, "You could've been born in Mississippi." Bilbo land. Theodore G. Bilbo, everyone swore, made Eugene Talmadge look like a bleeding-heart liberal when it came to hating blacks. Bilbo admitted to belonging to the KKK and was even quoted as saying, "Once a Ku Kluxer, always a Ku Kluxer." This was when Georgia's blacks conceded Mississippi's blacks had the better blues singers as, we felt, way down yonder in Bilbo land *was* the blues.

M adison wasn't the norm for Georgia, or the South, in race relations. If there was such a thing as "racial harmony" in a racially segregated town, then it existed in Madison. That is, with the exception of "Madison's Mad Man," a mean white policeman who served on the force from the late thirties into the early forties (but one who was mean to both blacks and whites ... except for his black mistress, who led him around by her apron strings).

Then there was the case of the Reverend Walter Mitchell Sr.

The Reverend Mitchell, black minister for many years of the county rural church of Smyrna, was an outspoken advocate of education for blacks. At the beginning of the fifties, he learned through an Atlanta educator friend that the state had appropriated funds to Morgan County black public schools (as well as other counties) in an effort to raise the standards of these classrooms closer to those of the local white schools. But in checking with the authorities at the county's black schools, none of them knew anything about any such appropriations.

Rounding up twenty-five black males, farmers who owned their land and other blacks independent of the white community, the Reverend Mitchell got them all to sign a petition, which he took to the county board of education. The petition requested that this state money be allotted to improving the local black schools as originally intended. To everyone's surprise, the board released the funds to upgrade black schools, including the construction of a new black high school in Madison.

But the Reverend Mitchell, while keeping close watch on the construction as it progressed, soon noticed that most of the school's facilities — the science lab, auditorium and restrooms — were being constructed in a much inferior manner to those that had been built at the white high school. Separate but *unequal.* Thus, the reverend protested. But this time he didn't get any backing from the original petitioners — they were not willing to push their luck with a white community busily putting up a *new* black high school.

The Reverend Mitchell's daughter, Rosalyn, who now lives in Atlanta with a family of her own and teaches at Morehouse College, recalls the threatening phone calls her father suddenly began getting once it was discovered he was now the lone black voice protesting the county school board's erection of a black high school inferior to the white high school. As the phone calls persisted, and got nastier, Rosalyn, a high school student at the time, remembers her determined father teaching her and her mother, Hazeltine, how to handle a shotgun in case their home was raided by these callers, which several of them kept threatening to do and the reverend inviting them to try it.

Then came the night he returned home from preaching in the nearby town of Monroe and discovered a car following his. The two cars were involved in a high-speed highway chase between Monroe and Madison that night. Shortly following this incident, he decided, for the safety of his wife and daughter, it was best he left his home of Madison and move to Atlanta.

But thanks to the Reverend Mitchell, Madison got a new black high school, along with buses to haul students to and

Novelist Raymond Andrews returns to the house in Morgan County where his family lived when he was a young boy. Those were times when he saw a South that a new generation of Southerners coming of age in more prosperous times never knew.

fro (during my Madison school days, only the white children rode a school bus). In the late seventies, the Reverend Mitchell returned to Madison to be honored by the NAACP for his fight for black education. The local ceremony was attended by the town's leading whites, including the mayor and members of the integrated county school board. The Reverend Mitchell has since died, but his memory lives on in his hometown of Madison.

(When I was growing up, there was talk that Madison's leading whites refused to let the Ku Klux Klan perform any whippings or lynching of blacks within the county. The bedsheeted brigade was told to keep their business outside of Morgan County. Thus nearby Monroe and Watkinsville became two favorite spots for the Klan to conduct their dirty business.)

There existed in Madison, and throughout Morgan County, an extremely strong sense of family and community among blacks. Scattered about the mostly agrarian (cotton) county were several small black farming communities, each with a church and a one-room schoolhouse. In some instances, the church served as the school, which was the way black education in the South got started following the end of slavery. Most of the early instructors were New England schoolteachers coming South to teach the freedmen ... and women. Each church was the heart of, and named for, its respective community. My family's church was, and still is, Plainview Baptist (most of the black churches were Baptist, except in the town of Madison, which had a Methodist and a Sanctified and two Baptist churches). Each church also had its own minister, or preacher. Most preachers, when not preaching, were farmers, carpenters or worked at other jobs mainly in the black community where they were leaders and mostly independent of whites. These ministers, the undertaker and the farmers who owned their own land were the few blacks whose life support didn't come directly from the white community.

Ministers have been the blacks' leaders going back to slavery, extending on down the ages from Monday Floyd to Martin Luther King (senior and junior), Adam Clayton Powell (senior and junior), Andrew Young, Jesse Jackson, et al. All rose from the pulpit. Perhaps in a freer society, these men, and many other blacks of their ilk, might've been drawn to and excelled in other fields. But in the black community of my youth, and before, there was no institution more powerful than the church, no individual role as important as that of church's head — the minister, God's man. (The undertaker had the most money, but the preacher had the flock.)

On Sundays, when people came to church, they came dressed in their very best. All during the week while working for the white folks, these grownups, regardless of how old or young they were, were called "boy," or "girl" by their employers. But at church, they were always "Mister," "Missis," "Brother" or "Sister." Here they were "Somebody." And the church *belonged* to us. It was *ours*. And God's. On occasion, a white person, or more, came to sit in the back of the congregation to, perhaps, enjoy the services. But undoubtedly in a reflex carried down from slavery when many escapes to freedom were planned in the church, we always felt the whites were there to "watch" us.

In the Madison of yore, whenever a black wanted a job above that of common laborer or servant work, then he, or she, had to leave town for the big city (usually Atlanta or the North) to try to find employment. This meant, upon finishing high school or upon entering adulthood, most young blacks left Madison, many out of a love for family and home — not wanting to go but given no choice. Just "leaving" was looked upon as being a success. Also, during the forties, most considered the best job to have in the white sector was the one held by the post office janitor, because working for the government meant security.

A year after Arnall was in the governor's office, I'd decided on becoming a movie star — a career that even ten-year-old me knew I had to leave Madison to pursue. This particular dream of mine I expressed to my mother, who carefully explained to me, while not trying to discourage me, that it was "extremely" hard for a black person to become a movie star (much harder than becoming a convict). But, she continued, whatever I wanted to be, I should always try my very best to be it, *never* give up trying and someday God would grant me my wish. Also, she pointed out with a finger, one thing for sure I had to always remember and *never* forget — that was whatever a colored person wanted to be in the white world, then he gotta be it better than a white person. I never forgot.

Even after blacks got the vote, right after World War II, there was no mad rush by most of them to get to the voting booths. Most of the Madison black voters I remember were schoolteachers, most of whom beseeched the students to, besides casting their ballots when they came of age, urge their parents to vote. But this last request was easier made than done. I never heard of any blacks in Madison being warned about voting, or registering to vote, by whites (though such could've been the case without my youthful knowledge). Because the Georgia newspapers apparently didn't find the subject matter too terribly interesting, we constantly heard and read (mainly from the black newspapers the *Chicago Defender* and the *Pittsburgh Courier*) what was happening to many other blacks throughout Georgia and the South for trying to register to vote, or vote, and that the practice of the majority of Morgan County blacks was to continue to stay away from the polls because the government, they felt, was still none of their business.

The first person in my family I can remember voting was my mother's sister who, in 1948, voted in the presidential election for Thomas Dewey, a Republican, because, she said, "The Democrats had never done anything for colored folks." Maybe not, but when her family, friends and enemies learned she'd voted "against" the party of Franklin Delano Roosevelt, they just shook their heads and blamed it on her having married a divorced man.

When integration eventually came to Madison (in the late sixties, after I had long gone), the local black leader in the forefront was not a preacher but nevertheless a churchman, Deacon George Williams Jr. of Plainview. He, along with his wife, Olivia, was instrumental in getting blacks hired in local, previously whites-only industries. These two also led the local black voter registration drive, along with helping integrate the county's schools. They were assisted by Mrs. Marie Bass Martin, a former teacher of mine, and the black high school principal at the time of integration.

And, I must add, integration of the schools went smoothly. Today, Deacon Williams, in his seventies but very much active, is now head of the county's Bi-Racial Committee, which consists of seven blacks and seven whites.

Meanwhile, Morgan County has three elected blacks in office now — two city councilmen and a county commissioner. The law enforcement department has provided several openings filled over the years by black policemen and sheriffs' deputies. A far cry from the day when Madison's Mad Man patrolled the streets "looking" for trouble. In addition, there is now an office of the NAACP in Madison.

In 1949, I left Madison and for the next thirty-five years lived in Atlanta, Washington, D.C., Chicago, New York City, Holland, Switzerland and a few other places (and in none of these did I become a movie star or a convict). But never did I lose contact with the town; I have relatives and friends living there, many having returned after years of living away. I still care for Madison and its people because I have many precious memories of the place, and to me it will always be home. Today I have no regrets about coming from the South because, by having been born and reared close to my American roots, I feel I gained, and retained, a deeper sense of self, family, community and history.

Having grown up in a racially segregated society and knowing nothing different, I accepted it at the time as being the Southern black's lot. After leaving the South, though, and looking back, there were times I got angry at having had many of my rights as an American citizen, and a human being, taken away. But most of all, I grieve for the many who were less fortunate than I. Segregation, I feel, hurt the young the most because black and white children never got together any place to form their own opinions of one another. Instead, they learned about the "other" race, or "them," through grown-ups ... who learned from grown-ups ... who learned ... ad nauseam — thus passing racial myths down through young mind after young mind.

Today's young Madison blacks aren't forced to leave town to find decent jobs because the entire area offers employment at the several industries operating in and around Morgan County. But, and most important, blacks can vote and run for local, state and national elective office, thus having more control over their own destinies. Now a great many young blacks, especially males, long leaders of the small Southern town exodus, are feeling a *part* of Madison and are staying home to live, work and raise families where they, and their ancestors, were born and grew up.

Walter Curtis Butler Jr., a second-term black county commissioner and former president of the local NAACP, lives in an attractive home in Madison with his wife and children. Butler was born in rural Morgan County and in 1962 graduated from Madison's then all-black high school. The Pearl Street school now serves as the middle (integrated) school (a modern gem that, in the early fifties, replaced the old, dilapidated Burney Street high school of my day).

Butler is a child of the civil rights age — that most optimistic period of black America's history. While listening to him talk about the local political scene, this optimism shines through because he shows no doubts of being a man very concerned about all the people of his county. This concern includes a fear that not enough of the local young blacks between the ages of twenty and thirty-five are showing the same interest and enthusiasm in government and politics that his generation did. He expressed the hope that this is only a phase and won't turn out to be a fact.

I know many blacks felt integration *itself* was going to be a "cure-all," while many whites felt it was going to be a "kill all." It's done neither. One has to *learn* that you *never* stop fighting for your rights. America is history's most competitive society, a society that too quickly and too easily chews up the less competent (black, white, yellow and red). Too much blood has been shed earning the right for blacks to compete equally within this fast lane for us to suddenly stop competing. These rights to compete in life's fast lane might not seem as equal to us in person as on paper. But they are *many* times over more equal today than they were in the American society Jackie Robinson, Martin Luther King Jr. and Frederick Douglass competed in. Yet they competed ... and well. ■

Tina McElroy Ansa

By her own description one of those textbook cases in the South, Tina McElroy Ansa grew up hearing stories and decided at the age of four or five that she, too, would become a writer, because she wanted to tell stories of her own. A native of Macon, Georgia, she entered journalism in 1971 after graduation from Spelman College in Atlanta and worked on the staffs of The Atlanta Constitution *and* The Charlotte Observer *before turning to full time freelance writing five years ago. For the past two years, she has devoted most of her time to writing a novel about a young girl with special powers growing up in a small Georgia town. Tentatively titled* Baby of the Family, *the book will be published next spring by Harcourt Brace Jovanovich Inc. Now living on St. Simons Island, Ms. Ansa says she did not always think of herself as Southern but experienced an epiphany while living in Baltimore during the early eighties. While not very distant from the South, she was far enough away, she recalls. "It was in Maryland," she has written, "that I learned how Southern I am. ... I dreamed of taking long car trips down red dirt roads that smelled rich and musty when a sudden cloudburst pounded them. I wanted to see the figure of a farmer way off in a field and blow my horn at him and see him raise his arm in an anonymous greeting. I yearned for a Georgia tomato." She cites other Southern women writers, especially Toni Morrison, Eudora Welty and Alice Walker, as powerful forces in her development.* ∎

Women in the Movement, Women and Men

Viewing the seven-part PBS documentary *Eyes on the Prize* was like watching old home movies of my family I'd seen over and over at every family get-together. But like most family members, I had seen the footage so often, I must have stopped paying attention to the details. As each week's installment rolled out images of life growing up in fifties and sixties in Georgia, I was enmeshed again in those times and shocked by what I saw.

The images on the television screen were the kind that go directly to the heart. The people were so familiar looking in a time-warp kind of way. It is always surprising to remember that just thirty years ago many adults wore hats to everyday functions, and women wore gloves and dresses to church and meetings. Few folks, even working country people, wore blue jeans except for field work. But something else surprised me about the brave people who put their lives and livelihoods on the line for their constitutional rights.

It was the number of women involved. Row after row, pew after pew, filled with women: old women, girls, teenagers, middle-aged matrons — all kinds of them in the audience of freedom meetings and rallies. That was not the only place I saw these soldiers of the movement. In news film, the overwhelming number of black people supporting the boycotting of segregated buses, the foot soldiers who walked to school and jobs and to the grocery store, were female. These were women who, like their male counterparts, put their jobs as maids and housekeepers in serious jeopardy by being bodacious enough to march, boycott, meet and protest.

I did not attend many rousing, inspiring church meetings where ministers and activists exhorted crowds of fervent freedom-seekers to stand up and demand equality. Macon, where I grew up, was certainly a part of the Deep South; in fact, it is the very heart of Georgia. But it was never the hotbed of the civil rights movement that other towns with more memorable names and campaigns — Selma, Birmingham, Albany, Wrightsville — were. But viewing some of the film documenting the movement, I had to ask, "Was I so caught up in the sweep of the movement that changed not only the face of the South and the entire country, but my own life that I didn't see the individual faces that made up the movement?"

I was struck over and over by the bravery, intelligence and sensitivity of these black women in standing up to white authority of the South. In Nashville, a college student named Diane, a mere girl dressed in her sleeveless sheath, stockings and flats, has the nerve to stand on the steps of City Hall with police officers and the national press surrounding her and other students and challenge the mayor himself to shake her hand, to be a human being. A black woman is thrown to the ground and beaten by a police officer in Alabama. We don't even know her name. Where did these women, young and old, get the guts, the daring will to do this: not just the well-known names such as Rosa Parks and Fannie Lou Hamer, but the other nameless female faces that flash on the television screen, the bodies in the crowd?

And more important, what happened to all that energy, that nerve when the movement marched on from the streets and schools and sit-ins of lunch counters and department stores and the voter registration booths to the political campaign trail? When the fight moved on to political as well as legal empowerment, what happened to these women?

The next logical step would be on to the political arena. It was the next step for many whose names became household words during the movement. Julian Bond, Andrew Young, Marion Barry, Charles Evers, Hosea Williams, Willie Brown. They all took that step to serve on city councils, in statehouses, in city halls, in the nation's Capitol. Jesse Jackson ran for president. What of the women?

The idea that black women just stepped back and let the men do their thing is not an easy notion to swallow. It gets caught in the throat like a chicken bone.

But the notion is there, nonetheless. And the numbers bear it out. Even in the last year, only twenty percent of black elected officials in the South were women — the smallest percentage of any region.

One woman who was a part of the Student Nonviolent Coordinating Committee contingent in Mississippi in the early sixties says she, like most women around her, spent her time typing, cooking, filing, encouraging citizens to register to vote, teaching classes, doing the nitty-gritty work that kept the voter registration-freedom campaign going in the South, while the leadership role — the high-profile, speaking, stirring-the-crowds roles — went, for the most part, to the men. And theirs were the faces that generations of voters became familiar with.

This visibility was essential in the forming of a politician. One woman remembered that the network news cameras covering the civil rights struggle didn't start rolling "till the men spoke."

And for all the stereotypes and images of loud-talking black women, speaking up in the South in the fifties and sixties was a very male domain. Many of the well-known men of the movement came out of the church or the tradition that encouraged young black men to speak out in a public forum and discouraged young women from doing the same. "Oh, you know, young Robert *speaks* so well. The boy is liable to be a minister or a school principal."

Many women of my generation privately snicker and

Tina McElroy Ansa

Ms. Ansa and her husband, Jonee Ansa, on their porch. Women of her generation didn't grow up in a matriarchal society, she said. Black fathers ruled their homes.

189

sneer when reading of the "matriarchal" society that has supposedly directed so much of their lives: strong black women holding the family together and making the decisions all alone with no help from the Absent Male. Many my age — in their late thirties and forties — don't remember a home where the women directed things. They remember a very different place, where women indeed did much of the work, but had little to do with the final decisions. A man usually did that, the decision-making, setting of the rules, enforcement of them, too. In my family, we children had to wait all day for punishment to be meted out, had to wait all day for "your father to get home" and his four-word order, "Go get the belt."

As with most things, the view of black women in the South depends on the perspective you have. For the most part, whites in the South saw black women only in their roles as maids, housekeepers, workers. To the white family, she was a figure of strength, stability, the fulcrum of some households where she worked. Her position as daughter, friend, wife and helpmate, mother and community member — roles that would have rounded out the view — never entered the picture.

The image has become legend even among black people, who should know better — so much so, that the strength and resilience of black women have become caricature characteristics. Even the tribute that hulking black football players pay to black women when they turn to the camera and mouth, "Hi, Ma!" contributes to that.

Perhaps it has been a heavier burden than readily realized, this assumption that black women, especially black Southern women, are stronger, more resilient, more reliable, more enduring — perdurable, in fact — than their Northern sisters, than their white counterparts, even than their men.

It is this assumption that has perhaps kept us black women doing the filing, the typing, the cooking, the marching, the canvassing, the nitty-gritty of the civil rights movement, putting our jobs as maids and teachers and cooks and house-keepers and nurses, our standing as good students on the line like the men who marched beside us. To be "the backbone" of the movement. Then, when the marching was over, to accept the generally accepted notion that it was time for us to go back to having babies and caring for them and getting a job to help feed the children and making sure their schooling and rearing and nutrition and morals were in order instead of taking to the stump and running for political office like so many of the most visible leaders of the movement did.

Many of the women who may have been thought of as political timber also directed their experience and verve to challenges less elite than the traditional political race. Look around any good-size city, and you'll find many of the people who are activists are black women who have channeled their energies into daily concerns: housing, day care, family health, community relations, employees' rights, the arts, food — the caring fields.

It seems too easy to dismiss the discussion by saying more black women didn't run for office because more women didn't have wives of their own to take care of the home front. (It's interesting to note, however, that there are a number of women who do hold public office who don't have *husbands*.)

And it is too facile an explanation to say merely that that's the way of our American culture. Women, forged by millennia of being told by everyone from St. Paul to Dear Abby to speak quietly, be a good helpmate, don't criticize your man, that it is the man's responsibility to earn the bacon, etc., have not taken to the forefront in many roles considered nontraditional.

But it is true that sexism affects all women, and the qualities so admired in a male worker of any kind — assertiveness, courage of your convictions, competitiveness, combativeness — are the very traits that are used to damn a woman aiming for the same prize.

One woman I know who was a SNCC worker in Georgia and Mississippi in her early twenties says there weren't that many women in the movement making speeches and rousing the audience. Some did and they stood out. But she points out that the audiences at most rallies were like the television cameramen and reporters. They were sitting there waiting for the "real" speakers, too.

I wonder why I haven't read all this before in some magazine or book. Of course, the late Septima Poinsette Clark's biography was published last year. And Mary King's memoir of her time in the movement is out. But she is white. And I hear there is a graduate student at Emory University looking into the subject for her thesis. But it seems so little for so prodigious a subject.

Perhaps it is not so surprising. Look at what's happening in the world of publishing. Some men of letters have taken to blaming black women for their recent and prolific spate of publishing, criticizing women writers for overshadowing black male writers and bumping them out of their book slots, basically by trashing black men. It is a divisive argument that leaves little room for discussion of how few books by blacks of either sex are actually getting published. It also ignores the years when the premier black writers in this country were Baldwin, Hughes, Cullen, Johnson, Wright, etc., and black women read those works with the fervor of mothers. Black female schoolteachers went out of their way, sometimes bucking school systems, principals and boards, to include the writings of these men in their classrooms.

The world of publishing, like the world of politics, isn't so different from our day-to-day world.

The stories are there. So are the questions. "I wonder what happened to Annie Divine in Canton, Mississippi? She was one who took political leadership. She was with the '64 Mississippi Freedom Democratic Party." "I think about Bertha Gober from Albany. She was a singer with the Freedom Singers of SNCC. She wrote a beautiful song called 'We'll

Never Turn Back.' I sure would like to know where she is." Those are questions from women who served in the movement — women who now work in everything from nursery schools to universities — about those who should have been the female Jesse Jacksons, the John Lewises, the Andrew Youngs. And these women wonder about the record of a movement that sometimes leaves them out altogether.

I hear it over and over, from women who, twenty-five years ago, faced down dog attacks, county sheriffs and irate employers. "I couldn't have stood up there in front of all those people then and stirred them. I couldn't have taken a leadership role," some say. "But I wouldn't think anything of doing that now. I guess it has to do with age."

I guess it does. Perhaps things are changing. The South certainly has changed. People change. Black mothers no longer discourage their daughters from wearing bright colors like red and no longer encourage them to let the man do all the talking. Perhaps like the South, black women's political ambitions have come of age.

But it's difficult not to mourn for all those women, those bodies in the crowd, who would have made such brave, fierce public servants. ■

James Alan McPherson

A sense of loss, it is often said, casts a long shadow over the Southern soul. But not every Southerner focuses on the same loss. For some, the Lost Cause remains a source of bitter nostalgia. For others, as concrete and asphalt encase red-clay and grassy fields, as families are sundered by movement and change, the dominant loss is a sense of place. Still others will tell you that the greatest loss has been the departure of whole generations of Southerners who found that only in leaving their home could they gain wholeness in life. Savannah native James Alan McPherson — winner of the Pulitzer Prize for fiction — confronted that experience early in this decade. Son of one of the first licensed black master electricians in the state, he earned a bachelor's degree at Atlanta's Morris Brown College in 1965 and went on to gain both a law degree at Harvard and a master of fine arts from the University of Iowa. From 1976 to 1981, McPherson taught at the University of Virginia. He is now a professor of English at the University of Iowa and considers himself a Southerner in exile, living away from a region that denies him a fully integrated life. A Guggenheim Fellow in 1972-73 and a MacArthur Fellowship winner in 1981, McPherson is the co-author of a book on railroads and author of two short-story collections, including Elbow Room, *which the Pulitzer Committee honored in 1978.* ∎

A Region Not Home: The View From Exile

I have a friend in Charlottesville, Virginia, a very principled and intelligent black woman named Margaret Cain. She is a lawyer. When I visited her office last October, I overheard her advising a black girl, a teenager, who had been encouraged by an older black man to cash a check he had forged. "You're going to jail," she told the girl.

Because I had once lived in Charlottesville and because I could recall from my own experience the hopelessness of the black American situation there, I could put together in my imagination all the tired conventions of the girl's story: a climate of greed, mendacity and self-interest that pervades much of American society; the general absence of moral clarity, especially for the young; the human need, almost always clumsily expressed among the poor, to *have* something; the gullibility of an adolescent girl looking for love and flattered by the attentions of an older man; the comic scene in which the girl, who is probably illiterate, presents the forged check to a constitutionally suspicious white clerk in a convenience store; her sentencing by a white criminal court judge who has been dehumanized by the endless procession of human failures paraded, or processed, daily through his court; the wasted and spirit-killing years in prison or in reform school; the frustration and sense of impotence of Margaret Cain and her partner, Earl Burton, two of the three black lawyers in Charlottesville, at another black life lost;

196

the resignation to their feudal state, or fate, on the parts of the masses of black people in Charlottesville, and their amazement over why Margaret Cain would dare try to make a difference; the same absence of care on the part of the white community; the profound isolation and depression of people like Margaret Cain.

"It has the potential to turn you into an animal," Earl Burton told me, the anger and frustration over so many years of losing uncomfortably close to the surface of his voice. I sat in Margaret Cain's office, listening to her advise the girl and sensed the part of me that is a lawyer being drawn into the tragedy I saw unfolding. I used my imagination to escape it. I thought about the three or four hours, at most, it would take me to fly home to Iowa City, Iowa.

I t is winter now in Iowa, where I live. The snow has settled in and hardened. The January cold is regular and comfortable. I have many friends here, black and white and other. Almost every day, people come by my house or call me up to invite me to dinner. I am confident that, here, I am first of all a person, a human being. I have been accepted into the life of the community. I have open and free and *easy* access to what in this community has meaning and value. I am secure. But since October, the image of the girl in Margaret Cain's office has come back to haunt me, has taken up residence within my private consciousness. Still, I have escaped being witness to the tragic facts of life that Margaret must confront each day, and I have found a relative peace. I read books, teach students, talk about how things *should* be, mostly with people who agree with me. A good number of my students since I have settled here have been white Southerners. At first I thought it strange that they would seek me out, that they would enroll in my classes. Now I am satisfied that, in Iowa at least, we share the same situation. I am in exile here, plain and simple. But like black Americans anyplace, here my Southern white students are viewed as members of a different culture. They come to my classes for the same reason I came to Iowa: to find open and free and *easy* access to what in this environment is meaningful. I understand part of the cultural context of their fiction. They seem to feel as secure under my instruction as I feel living in Iowa.

I do not flatter myself that the South cannot endure without a handful of writers and intellectuals. Just now, the civic religion of the entire country seems to be money — the getting and the manipulation and the worship of it — and writers and intellectuals in all regions find themselves isolated, talking only to each other. I imagine there is already an overabundance of native-born Southerners, black and white, who are eager to participate in the region's economic development and its evolving political life. The South already has within its borders most of the black resources it needs to enhance its image and consolidate its economic and political power. But it does seem to me, when I look back on my own generation of black Americans, those who were born in the early forties and who benefited from the earliest stirrings of the civil rights movement, that the region has lost some of its best people, and the Margaret Cains and Earl Burtons of the small towns of the South have lost valuable mentors.

Many of the most successful of my college classmates, members of an older generation, now live outside the region. They have sidestepped most of the daily battles that the younger black professionals must continue to fight. They have not escaped racism, but they have moved to places where they are free enough from those distracting battles to devote most of their energies to professional goals. The relative security of their lives allows them to maintain the belief that they are strictly middle class, as opposed to symbolic pawns in the uniquely American uncertainty over what constitutes class and what constitutes caste. They do not have the time or the energy to have their self-worth defined, or redefined, by shifts in the political mood of the country. I am thinking of those who were my classmates at Morris Brown College in Atlanta more than twenty years ago, of Edward Halman, now a high-level bureaucrat in Washington, D.C.; Robert Morgan, now a doctor in Los Angeles; Ira Kemp, now a lawyer in Philadelphia; Steve Womack, now a lawyer in Paterson, New Jersey; Freddy Thomas, now a teacher someplace. I think now of all of them, and I wonder what differences we might have made in the total fabric of Southern life if we had returned to our respective home-towns and had been able to stand, as peers and as mentors, beside the younger Margaret Cains and Earl Burtons. But for us, the moment of decision passed more than a generation ago, and now a new generation is slowly making some of the same decisions. It is to the credit of the South that a great deal has changed since the time when my age group saw migration as the only option.

My own peers now are writers and intellectuals, black and white. I have had to struggle all my life to find them. It is a difficult thing for anyone to develop an orientation toward books, toward the life of the mind, in an environment that has a predetermined sense of what is "correct" and what is not, of what ideas are of value and what ideas are not. For such people as a whole, cosmopolitan areas traditionally have served as havens, where the life of the mind is assigned a certain value. I remember being among the first to take advantage of the Atlanta Public Library after it was integrated in 1963. I remember being slapped by a white man on the street outside the library. For many years, I believed that this enraged white man slapped me because I am black. Now I think it might have been because I was black *and* carrying a stack of books and several paintings away from the library. I also remember my first tour of Harvard Square in Cambridge, Massachusetts, in 1965, and my joy at viewing the number of bookstores, and my amazement at the number of people who stood around in them, shamelessly reading

James Alan McPherson belongs now to the world of books. But twenty-five years ago, a white man slapped him for using the public library.

books. Within the black community of Savannah, Georgia, during my formative years, there were no such places. Over the years, in a variety of circumstances, I have found people who share my interest. Many of them are white.

Because of the relatively small number of book-reading and book-writing black Americans, such adjustments traditionally have been the case. And those black Americans who are deeply involved with books have usually found peers outside of the South. But for a period of years during the seventies, years when I was teaching in Cambridge, in California, in Baltimore, there seemed a possibility that black intellectuals would be welcomed back to the South to take part in the region's conversation with itself. This long moment of reconsideration lasted until the early eighties. And then something happened. Hodding Carter III was one of the few to articulate the new mood, and his reflections did not appear until January 1986, in *Playboy,* of all places. "There are my occasional visits home," he noted in an article on the revival of racism, "when old friends speak despairingly of renewed race hatred on both sides, of polarization and separation to a degree unknown for twenty years." Like many black Americans who had been invited to return home, I found myself, during those years written about by Hodding Carter, trying to understand intellectually what was essentially a blood lust for a return to a past in which I was not supposed to exist. The climate was most threatening, and most painful, in the smaller towns of the South. I found myself isolated, examined, assigned a role as an inferior, as a thing. Rather than attempt to live under such conditions, I chose exile from the entire region as a matter of principle.

But to my surprise, here in Iowa, many other Southerners joined me. They were young white writers and intellectuals, mostly from the smaller cities and towns: Leigh Wilson from Tennessee; Jane Tressel from Virginia; Tom Jenks from Virginia; Bob Schacochis from Virginia; Daniel Woodrell from Mississippi by way of Missouri; David McFarland from Alabama; Mark Franks from Oxford, Mississippi;

Breece Pancake, dead now of suicide, from West Virginia; Beth Filson from Georgia; June Wagner from Florida; Donald Seacrest from North Carolina; Patricia Foster from Alabama; Judy Bouvier from Texas; Grover Ellis from Texas; Tom Bailey from West Virginia; Jim McCulla from West Virginia; Louise Blum from Georgia; Mike Lankford from Texas and Oklahoma; Chris Holbrook from Kentucky. From daily interactions with these white Southerners, from their recognition of my place in their world and from my recognition of their place in mine, I had confirmed for myself once again that the private selves of writers and intellectuals are integrative, even when regions are not.

I have learned from my students. I have learned some invaluable things about the "white" South and its relation to the "black" part of itself. I have grown confident that part of my sensibility is sufficiently Southern to make the students feel comfortable working with me. I try my best to make them feel secure in my classes. Perhaps in exchange for this, they have taught me something about the paths that led each of them to Iowa. They have given me insights into the symbolic role assigned to people like me by the white South. They have given me access to the other side of the story. And I have learned from them that in running away, we were more alike than different.

It is a commonplace observation that the major cities of the South, and most especially Atlanta, have changed a great deal since the sixties. They have begun to follow the evolutionary process of every cosmopolitan area evolving the social forms that allow for external coexistence between people from a variety of social and racial groups. The impetus behind this evolutionary process is almost always economic. In the major economic centers such as Atlanta, an attempt has been made to establish a transcendent jurisprudence or a set of civic values over a broad range of ethnic groups. This jurisprudence makes for tolerance and cohesiveness and for an acceptance of diversity as a norm. But a comparable evolutionary process has not yet taken place in the smaller towns, where the economic impetus has halted or has slowed or has never begun. The rampant materialism of the eighties has not enhanced, and has very often retarded, the development of transcendent values in both city *and* small town in all parts of the country, the South included. But it is within the towns that the old tensions still exist, and where the values of the past live just beneath the surface of daily life. They are likely to re-emerge during times of economic uncertainty or when the movements of the country's political life suggest, even faintly, a movement back toward the past.

What resides in that past, my students have taught me, is a Southern sense of inferiority — morally, because of black slavery; militarily, because the region lost the Civil War; and culturally, because the region speaks and thinks in different ways. I have learned that, in that past, black people were viewed as the cause of many of the region's problems and that a residual bitterness toward my group still exists and can be overtly expressed during times of economic and political uncertainty. I have learned that if a black person leaves the area in response to overt expressions of hostility, the gesture can be viewed as a slap in the face, as an insult. I have learned that most of the smaller towns still maintain a narrow range of acceptable ideas and through this process have refined a simplified code of behavior that is considered "correct." This code allows little deviance for *anyone*, white or black, male or female. There is little room for the complex human being. The entire system is administered by those who do the "correct" things, and through their somewhat gallant assumptions of what is right and "correct," the aberrant or humanly complex person is either put back into place or else guided to the nearest exit. Most important of all, I have learned that there has been a strong tradition in the small towns of the South of exporting its writers and intellectuals, its complex people, to more hospitable regions, so much so that in recent years, the more evolved areas of the South have had to *import* teachers and thinkers from other regions and from other cultural groups. But very often, even within the cities, these newcomers do not share the same traditions of native-born Southerners. And the fearful perception of native white Southerners that they are being displaced in their own region leads to increased bitterness against the traditional scapegoats: black Southerners.

These are the traditions of the Southern past as my students have taught them to me. They are the traditions that have resurfaced during the Reagan years. They have caused a great many personal problems for my white Southern students. Accepting this, I know now that my own problem, which is in part a racial one, is irrevocably intertwined with theirs. We are all looking for a place to return to, a place where we can feel secure. The major commercial cities of the South, with their building energies, do offer havens of a kind, but they are not yet our homes, and small towns can be lonely places for people of the mind. I receive letters all the time from my white Southern students. Only a few have returned to their hometowns. The others are still on the road. Even as I was writing this, I received a call from an aspiring writer in Kentucky, who lives, he said, "just over the mountain from Milton, West Virginia, where Breece Pancake lived." He wanted me to read his work and complained that he had no one in his community to show it to.

Here in Iowa City, we Southerners have gone through crises together, have eaten together, have gotten drunk together, have shared intimate details of our personal lives. Our exchanges have been rich and heartfelt and deep. Here my white students do not intimate to me that they feel superior or inferior to me. We have struck an emotional and intellectual balance. We have become friends. It may be that the imperatives of a common cultural background became more pronounced once we were cut off from the institutional pressures that kept our racial identities paramount. I like to think that within such receptive small towns as Iowa City, we have managed to negotiate a quiet integration between our inner selves and our outward actions. I like to believe that, despite all our differences and personal problems, we have achieved a certain safe degree of integrity.

Last April, I had the beginnings of a mild stroke just at the end of one of my classes. I asked Mark Franks, a Mississippian, to drive home with me. But as I began bleeding more and more, Mark took the wheel and rushed me to the emergency room of a hospital. He kept saying, "Oh, Lord, something *broke!* Oh, Lord, this is *bad!*" He watched over me as the doctors and nurses tried to stop my bleeding. Vaguely aware of him in the background of the emergency room, I wanted to say, "Oh Lord, this is *good!*" Mark Franks cares for people. Over a period of two years, I had observed him going against his immediate self-interest to help those people, white *and* black, who needed him. He added that his actions toward me would have been the same if the bleeding had occurred in the Mississippi Delta. I would trust my life to Mark Franks' sense of integrity anyplace in the world. Oxford, Mississippi, has sustained a loss because Mark has moved, first to Iowa, then to Montana. What will it take for his hometown to attract him back?

In any healthy community, there ought to exist a way to achieve a balance between the two basic human needs for security and integrity. The complex human being should not have to run from community to community in order to find, or to create, the security he needs in order to be himself. I believe that this is all the Southern "racial" problem comes down to: allowing the necessary changes in the social fabric that will permit black Southerners to exist, and to grow, as human beings. But speaking as a writer and as a teacher who has learned from his Southern white students, I know that something more is required of any community that takes in people like us. We require that the basic moral assumptions of the community be clear enough in their expression toward such "complex" people that those people can feel secure in their reliance on them. We insist on our right to be complex and to be defined as something more than "eccentrics." We require that our individuality be treated with respect, that we be accepted as the people of integrity that we are. This means that any small town that invites us in has to recognize the difference between collective and individual codes of conduct.

In this respect, I am fortunate. The block on which I live contains people from almost every "racial" group in the world. The university at which I teach has pledged itself to making such diversity the norm within its classrooms.

But could those of us who have struggled here in Iowa to know each other transfer to our home communities *outside* the commercial cities of the South the same degree of mutual support, tolerance and acceptance of the humanly complex "other"? Would sufficient room be made for us to provide an alternative that is acceptable? Would my students be allowed to mature into functional alternatives instead of being dismissed as mere eccentrics? Would the social forms of the city, the spirit of external coexistence, be allowed to penetrate the refined internal world of the small town? I do not know. I know that while I have security and a small degree of integrity here in Iowa City, I do not have the solid kind of integrity that comes from attempting to be oneself within communities that consider such people eccentric. I do not have to struggle every day, like Margaret Cain, to maintain, against impossible odds, an integration between my inner self and my outward actions. Like Mark Franks, I have found an easy refuge in the territories outside the South. But I think sometimes that I would like at least to observe, and perhaps translate into fiction, the tragic *efforts* of people like Margaret and Earl. I know for certain that the quality of intellectual discourse, in all parts of the South, has been impoverished because the region has lost so many of its complex people. They might have done much to influence the civic values of the South, city and small town. In order to live freely in the region, however, even outside of the protective enclaves provided by the cities, people like me would have to believe that we would be treated as complex human beings and not as symbols whose value is contingent upon fluctuations in the political climate. Speaking personally, my own sense of security within *any* community would have to come from my belief that my winning a Pulitzer Prize and a MacArthur Fellowship, after having worked my way off the welfare rolls of Savannah, are not actions that are "wrong" or "incorrect" or that make other people uncomfortable.

I speak now for myself and in part for the white Southern students I have taught here. It seems to me that it is now the responsibility of this younger generation of white Southerners from the small towns of the region, backed by commercial and evolutionary processes emanating from the major cities, to encourage the consolidation of a pragmatic alternative within the small towns of the South. The young people ought to be encouraged, in the most public and meaningful ways, to try again to make the necessary changes in the social fabrics of their inward-looking home communities. They ought to be encouraged to *insist* that their human complexity be assigned the status of a valid alternative. They ought to be encouraged to return home, not to the nearest cities, but to the small-town worlds that first nurtured them. They ought to be celebrated as the first agents of change, the human links between the culture of the cities and the culture of the towns. I speak here of goodhearted people, people like Mark Franks who carry emotional equipment that is needed for the revival of the social forms that have been damaged by the Reagan years. It may well be that if enough of them returned and worked with the younger generation of black and white Southerners, a quiet kind of transformation might be resumed. Just a few small towns, under the nurturance and protection of more evolved cities, areas that welcome difference as a valid alternative, might go a long way toward developing a cultural climate that would encourage the region's complex and creative people to remain at home. Such areas might also attract back some of the people who have already settled in other regions. Such efforts, given the commercial prosperity of the major cities of the South, should not be that difficult, and they might help the South reclaim its native-born talent as a way of easing some of the tension caused by the importation of "outsiders." This would require all regions of the South to recognize the complexity of the familiar as a first step toward recognizing the complexity of the "foreign." Considering the great variety of "foreigners" now abroad in the world, would it be so high a price to pay? I am reminded that the very first attempt at integration in Western tradition began with the attempt to encourage the country towns to consider the values of the city. The institution of the nation-state resulted from this effort. What new social forms, far beyond the outdated notion of the nation-state, would the American South evolve, given its creative potential?

When I left Charlottesville almost seven years ago, I brought with me to Iowa a principle, one I have tried my best to generalize in my dealings with all people, but most especially with my students. It is what I have come to believe is the spiritual essence of Thomas Jefferson's principle, and it has more to do with the life of the human soul than with politics: "We hold these articles of faith to be the revealed truth: All *souls* are created equal and they are endowed by God with certain inalienable rights, among which are immortality, free will and access to grace." I think sometimes that it is the absence of any widespread belief in the immortality of the human soul, of a life after this present one, that is responsible for so much decadence and greed and meanness in contemporary American life. I suspect that the substitution of money and its limited power for a transcendent principle is the root cause of the spiritual decay that has eroded the meaning of what was once an American civic religion. I wish, sometimes, that the South could harness its strong tradition of evangelism, in a very gentle way, to the spiritual essence of Jefferson's principle. The region and the rest of the country are in great need of a meaningful spiritual civility.

In the meantime, Margaret Cain and Earl Burton still sit isolated in their small law office in Charlottesville. It seems to me that the goodhearted people like them have inherited many of the complex human problems on which the political and moral culture of the eighties defaulted. Because so many, many people have abandoned them during the material excesses of this decade, they have become reluctant heirs to the limited moral legacy of this decade. They have shouldered an obligation no one could have forced upon them. And in doing that, they are achieving a special kind of nobility, one not based on wealth or blood or social status. It is based on doing more than most other people would to maintain something that is right and good.

I think that Mark Franks, now struggling against these winter months out in Montana, is another of these special kind of people. There are grains of gold in their hearts. I hope that one day Margaret and Mark and Earl will meet each other, and recognize each other, on the soil of the homeplace. I want to believe that when enough such people are secure in their places of origin, in the small towns of the South, to resume the hard work of revitalizing the social fabric, it will be a signal to all the other wanderers that a choice has been made. And it will be a challenge, a gauntlet thrown down, for the wanderers to return *home* and renew the struggle to redefine our obligations to each other as a common people.

For my own part, I will be in Iowa, in the Territory, waiting for such signals. ■

VI.

Life and Literature

Josephine Humphreys

A native of Charleston, South Carolina, Josephine Humphreys was encouraged to become a writer in her teens by her grandmother. The child of a prominent family, including a great-great-grandfather who was the Confederacy's secretary of the treasury, she studied writing with the influential North Carolina novelist Reynolds Price at Duke University, earned a master's degree in English at Yale and was pursuing a doctorate at the University of Texas when she married. Before her celebrated, but delayed, debut as an author in her mid-thirties, she taught literature and remedial English at the Baptist College in Charleston. Focusing on the changing social structure in her native city, her first novel, Dreams of Sleep, *told the tale of a family that holds out against the tide in an area undergoing redevelopment. It won the Ernest Hemingway Foundation Award in 1985. Two years later, Ms. Humphreys further demonstrated her understanding of the human relationships in the New South in* Rich in Love, *a novel focusing on a season of domestic discontent in a suburban South Carolina community. She was also a contributor to* A World Unsuspected: Portraits of Southern Childhood, *published in 1987. Though rooted like so many Southern writers by a sense of place, she has witnessed a shift — as small Southern towns and rural areas are engulfed by urban sprawl — that sometimes seems closer to a nightmare than to a dream fulfilled.* ∎

A Disappearing Subject Called the South

To tell the truth, the South is once again in ruin.

Our first ruin — slaves let loose and mansions burnt — ought to have been a fortunate fall, the kind of collapse that clears an old bad life for new good things. But we are here again, witness to a second devastation, and not only witness, but party. We have done it to ourselves.

I am talking about visible ruin — the real physical destruction of our places. Let us call it, for purposes of irony, "development." Development is the dirty family secret of the South, and, like most dirty secrets, it is known to everyone.

A writer friend from Florida tells me that one can't really write about Southern development anymore. The topic is stale. Too many writers have milked the condo-golf resort scene; too many books have pointed out that the South continues to become more like the North every day. Maybe so, I say; but stale news may still be true and urgent. Recently I drove through the urban labyrinth of Charlotte, North Carolina, with a Yankee writer, and after studying the scenery for an hour, which is how long it takes to get from one side of Charlotte to another, he finally said, "Nothing prevents this from being New Jersey."

Nothing prevents it. That is why, no matter how overworked the topic, we must continue to write about development. We must prevent it. Writers in particular have a duty to prevent it, because for us what's at stake is lifeblood.

There's a peculiar relationship between fiction and place, one that is rehashed daily in literary seminars; it remains peculiar and fascinating. Fiction must *take place*. Without what Shakespeare called "a local habitation," there can be no good narrative, only "airy nothing," a poor brain's fiddling. But whenever story can locate itself in reality, it will draw on reality's mystery and power, becoming that oddity of literary endeavor, true fiction. This geographical imperative exists because fiction has as its natural subject the real world and real man in it, and all the complications brought on by one clear fact: *We are here.* The writing of fiction must always involve both the *we* and the *here*.

The writing imagination is fueled by real places. A writer living in Disney World, like the last of the dusky seaside sparrows, would be so removed from his real original home that fiction (true fiction as opposed to its opposite, pure romance) would become impossible. In the past, the South had a vast supply of real places. But the first gradual and now swift metamorphosis of our geography has changed our literature.

We have, of course, already lost our original home, the Eden of the great forests, swamps, rivers, islands, mountains. What's left now are tiny pockets, museums of artificially sustained wildness run by the Park Service. Southern writers have felt the loss. In William Faulkner's Yoknapatawpha County it looms, a constant awareness of paradise surrendered to sawmills and plantations and towns. Here is the so-called "sense of loss" that is said to characterize Southern fiction. It is not that we lost a war. It is that we lost our place. We must forget the Southern wilderness; it is as finally gone as a lost love, and nothing but pain to recall.

But towns! Towns are another matter. Towns are what I grieve for now. The natural setting of Southern fiction is not wilderness, nor farm nor city. It is town. For the most part, that is where our fictional vision has been focused; that is the place that has seemed most fitting for the kinds of stories we have wanted to tell — narratives of the human community. While one life may form the spine of a novel, one life alone is not enough in a Southern novel. Our subject is the concert of human lives.

We've never really had a strong tradition of literary individualism. No Southern Thoreau has emerged to celebrate the individual Southern consciousness. Maybe Jefferson's voice was one early solo trumpet, but Jefferson's overriding concern was still with society, how men must live together. In fiction, there has been no Southern *Moby Dick,* no novel so thoroughly stripped down to the single mind and its mad, glorious quest. Our best match for Melville is Poe, not a novelist at all.

Supposing Mark Twain to be the first great Southern novelist (and incidentally the greatest American novelist), I see our early need to re-create the South and show it to the rest of America as well as to ourselves. To wish to do so is not necessarily apology. We are a self-conscious region, suffused with the kind of inwardly turned interest that accompanies a sense of separateness. We've never really felt American. We've always tried to show why.

The easiest and truest answer is the long-lived disaster of slavery; I would say it is the only answer necessary, except that I always feel there is something more, some schism of mind and soul that pre-dated slavery, that maybe even enabled it. All my life in the white South, I have heard apologists diminish the importance of slavery: It was not a direct cause of the Civil War; it was a system that actually benefited the slaves; it was an economic necessity and therefore excusable. But the human mind, while it can superficially deceive itself, has a deep knowledge of moral truth. True crime against nature — like slavery or development — cannot be committed unknowingly. An entire society may, for a time, look the other way, but at heart it will know the truth. Its writers will tell that truth, sooner or later. They will maneuver for a good view of society, and they will tell what they see. Their best vantage point will be a town.

A purely rural setting is hard ground for the novelist;

Josephine Humphreys

Born and raised in Charleston, a city that treasures its past, Josephine Humphreys sits on the front porch of her antebellum house on Society Street, in the center of the city. The destructive effect of urban redevelopment was a theme of her first novel.

217

more often than not, he'll widen the rural scope by taking his people to town now and then, or by hauling in travelers. But a purely urban setting is hard, too, because community itself is not to be seen in most cities; the proportions of the place have gotten out of hand and are no longer of human scale. Town alone is that community in which community itself is discernible.

Reynolds Price has said that fiction is best set in a town of fewer than ten thousand souls, "a town from whose center open country [can] be reached by a fifteen-minute walk." He goes on to give the reason: fiction's deep need for a vision of the permanent beauty of the world. The city, he says, can mostly support only "bad poems and novels full of neon light on wet asphalt, unshaven chins, scalding coffee at four a.m."

There's something else, too. Something happens there, at that spot imagined by Price, the place where you can see the end of town. At that margin, the mystery of human community and the mystery of non-human beauty touch. A street dead-ends in a cornfield. The last garden fence keeps out thicket and vine, and a railroad track curves off into woodsy nowhere. Even sounds stop, fly into thin air. Stand there awhile, where you can see both town and no-town, and you will know something about life on Earth. You will know enough for a novel.

Where I live, in the South Carolina Low-country, towns are hard to see. Some, like Mount Pleasant, have been swallowed whole by neighboring cities. Some, like Summerville, have spread themselves outward to link up with a neighboring spreading town, and the original boundaries of both have been lost. The perfect town of McClellanville is being colonized, its edges blurred by a slow accretion of new houses. For the fullest sense of community, shouldn't a person be able to see the limits of his settlement? If he can't see the end of his town, won't he have a diminished notion of home, and no notion of an unknown territory beyond home?

In parts of the South, we are actually building fake towns. Places called "Seaside" and "Charleston Place" in Florida are merely developments costumed as towns. A real town is the work of a kind of collective dream, the sum of a thousand individual urges belonging to real people: the urge to love, to form families, to educate and worship and fight and eat and invent. The new fake towns signal our desperate need for town, but they do not fill it. They are "quaint" in the original sense of the word: wrought with skill, clever. I see a parallel tendency in our fiction, the increasing output of "Southern" works set in a "South" that can't be found in reality or even in history, an exaggerated and quaint fake place.

There are, of course, still Southern towns. I have seen them — set out to see them, in fact, on a journey that took me looping from South Carolina through northern Georgia, Alabama, Mississippi, and Louisiana to Texas (where I figured I could make out the limits of the South itself) and then back along the coastal route into Florida, and home. They still exist, places like Talladega, Alabama, and Jefferson, Texas, two of the loveliest.

But I had the feeling all along that these towns too were endangered. I had the feeling that one day the Southern town may exist only as a town-museum, its houses precious objets d'art, its "way of life" annually re-enacted in period costume. Some are already approaching that museumized condition. Talladega's houses are marked with plaques and listed with the National Register of Historic Places. Jefferson has come under the sway not of the National Register but of a thriving bed-and-breakfast enterprise, which also labels its houses. These towns and others like them have discovered that tourists will come, and will pay, to see what a real town looks like.

But once a town is museumized, it loses the very authenticity that tourists enjoy and writers crave. Its useful force as a real place dissipates. I don't predict what will happen to our fiction when writers can no longer put themselves in touch with that force. But I suspect that we will depend more and more on the "South" as setting, where there may be antebellum houses and Spanish moss and horse-drawn carriages, but where there is no community.

Our better writers may then turn to the secret towns, those that are still real because no one wants to develop them, or even lay eyes on them: the poor towns like Tchula, or Indian towns like Pearl River, in Mississippi; towns hidden within cities, like Prichard, Alabama, inside Mobile; and the nightmare migrant towns of Belle Glade and Immokalee in Florida. Nothing picturesque or festive or quaint or even comfortable here. These are real places, with more force and more story and more community than any of our developed places. *We are here,* in Pearl River, in Tchula, in Belle Glade. We are still here, and from here may again reconstruct ourselves.   ■

Louis D. Rubin Jr.

Although one of the leading authorities on Southern literature in academia, University of North Carolina English Professor Louis D. Rubin Jr., has not been content to limit himself to teaching and writing criticism. The South Carolina native also has published the works of Southern writers as president of Algonquin Books, a publishing house that began in his home in Chapel Hill in 1982. Among the talents he has introduced are Jill McCorkle and Clyde Edgerton. A founding member of the Fellowship of Southern Writers, former associate editor of the Richmond News Leader *and author of two novels, he served as general editor of* The History of Southern Literature, *which was acclaimed as the most extensive work of its kind in three decades when published by the Louisiana State University Press in 1985. In the introduction he wrote, "The facts are that there existed in the past, and there continues to exist today, an entity within American society known as the South, and that for better or worse the habit of viewing one's experience in terms of one's relationship to that entity is still a meaningful characteristic of both writers and readers who are or have been a part of it." At a conference on the region's literature last year, Rubin reiterated that theme. "They say there is no such thing as Southern writing, that it's just a form of local chauvinism. But can you imagine a meeting like this being held on Rocky Mountain writing?"* ∎

Changing, Enduring, Forever
Still the South

*I*s today's so-urban South still "Southern"?
If an author is described as a "Southern"
writer, does it still mean anything
important?

Whenever questions like those are
asked, I think of a certain morning in Atlanta about eighteen
years ago. The Regency-Hyatt House, as it was then called,
had only recently opened and, with its immense open atrium, blue dome, glassed-in interior elevators and general
quality of gaudy dazzlement, was like nothing ever seen anywhere else.

We were in town for a convention of teachers of literature, and several of us went over to see it. We were properly
impressed. As the latest jewel of opulence in a Southern city
that for a century and more had been renowned for its
wealth and up-to-dateness, the new hotel appeared to exemplify all that was new and glittering and expensive in our
part of the country. What used to be known as the Pellagra
and Hookworm Belt, America's Economic Problem Number
One, the Benighted South, the Bible Belt, the Sahara of the
Bozart, and so on, was now being called the Sun Belt, and
the Regency-Hyatt seemed appropriately its symbol.

We watched for a while, then walked back toward Five
Points. As we passed in front of the Federal Building, we
heard someone shouting. On the corner was a young man,
red-haired, red-faced, seemingly in his late twenties or early
thirties. He was attired in a cheap, awkwardly fitted grey

suit, and he was calling upon the populace of Atlanta to re-
pent, for the Day of Judgment was at hand. That nobody was
paying the slightest attention to him seemed to daunt him
not at all. At the top of his voice, heedless of the absence of
an audience, he articulated his dire message to the unbe-
lieving city.

Because we were literary people, we recognized at once
that what we were seeing was the living incarnation of Hazel
Motes, the self-appointed evangelist in the late Flannery
O'Connor's novel *Wise Blood,* who came from rural Georgia
to preach to the complacent, godless citizenry of Atlanta.

Moreover, in the contrast between the appearance of the
red-haired young evangelist and what he was doing and the
astoundingly ornamented and lavish hotel we had just been
viewing, there was a kind of parable involved. One of my
companions, the late C. Hugh Holman, even wrote an essay
about it, which he titled "The View From the Regency-
Hyatt."

For was not that evangelist the living embodiment of pre-
cisely that rural-dominated, Christ-haunted, racially segre-
gated, poverty-stricken South that by the seventies had sup-
posedly disappeared in favor of the Sun Belt? And did not
the active presence of that young man on a street corner in
downtown Atlanta, not many blocks from the blue-domed
and fabulous new hotel, reproduce the cultural contrast and
conflict that lie at the heart of the literature of the South in
our century: the tension between the old and the new, be-
tween past and present, between change and resistance to
change?

That the South, as it has been, is about to disappear has
been a commonplace of thinking about the region for much
longer than a century. The historian George B. Tindall wryly
lists a lengthy series of economic, social and political devel-
opments that were supposed to signify the demise of the
South: Swift westward expansion, too much easy money in
the Cotton Kingdom, the development of railroads, Seces-
sion, the loss of the Civil War, the end of slavery, the Recon-

struction, Populism and the rise of the Wool Hat Boys, the advent of the automobile and the construction of a network of highways linking the countryside to the cities, mass communications, the impact of industrialization, the leveling process of the Depression, World War II, post-war prosperity, the Brown v. Board of Education decision, television, the end of legal segregation in public accommodations, the spread of suburbia, the one man-one vote dictum, the end of the one-party system, etc. — each has been regarded as sounding the death knell for the Southern Way of Life.

Yet here we are, a century and a quarter after the burning of Atlanta and the fall of Richmond, still arguing about it and still predicting it. For the argument even to arise, it follows that there must still be certain aspects about life in the South that have managed to survive and remain distinctive, so that the prospect of their imminent disappearance can either be lamented or praised, depending upon one's attitude.

It also follows that insofar as the word "Southern" in front of the word "fiction" has any meaning other than merely geographical, there must be elements common to most of the novels, stories, etc., written by Southern authors that make them identifiable as such, and that enough such elements persist to prompt us to argue whether they are finally on the way out.

What are those distinctive "Southern" elements, reputedly common to literature in the South whether written by William Faulkner or Eudora Welty, Margaret Mitchell or Flannery O'Connor, Richard Wright or Ernest Gaines, Allen Tate or James Dickey, or whoever was writing?

They are usually said to be a distinctive awareness of the Past, a firm identification with a Place, a preoccupation with one's membership in a community, a storytelling bent (as compared with a concern for Problems), a strong sense of family and an unusually vivid consciousness of caste and class, especially involving race. No one writer's work may

University of North Carolina English Professor Louis D. Rubin Jr., cradling his cat Gus at his Chapel Hill home, sees the changing South as a continuing source of new literature.

stress all of them, and of themselves they are by no means unique to Southern writing, but their common presence, and their continuing mutual action upon each other, have been the hallmarks of the Southern novel.

Now if the South as we know it is speedily disappearing, and if the forces that have shaped its experience in the past — poverty, rurality and isolation, segregation, the Confederate heritage, the one-party system, fundamentalist religion and so on — and caused its literary imagination to take the forms noted above are either going or gone, then those characteristics should be largely missing from the work of the younger Southern authors who grew up in the years following World War II.

Well, are they? To ask the question is to answer it: certainly not. For anyone who is familiar with the work of younger Southern authors such as not only Josephine Humphreys but also Alice Walker, Jill McCorkle, Anne Tyler, Clyde Edgerton, Gail Godwin, Pat Conroy and James Alan McPherson knows just how important those ingredients remain in their fiction. They are handled *differently*, but they continue to give form to the literary imagination of Southern writers.

Let me cite only one example. Jill McCorkle, whose novel *Tending to Virginia* was so widely and favorably reviewed when it appeared last fall, was raised in Lumberton, North Carolina, a small town, but one located along Interstate 95, and with shopping malls and 7-Elevens instead of general stores. Jill McCorkle never saw a Confederate veteran, much less talked with one. She watched the same television programs as did youngsters in Pittsburgh, Chicago and Denver. She graduated from a state university with twenty thousand students, took a graduate degree at Hollins College, has lived in North Carolina, Virginia, New York and Florida, and currently resides in Massachusetts.

Yet in *Tending to Virginia,* four generations of women from the same family have an impact upon each other. In order for the youngest woman, who is expecting a child soon, to understand who she is and why, she must find out about the experience of her mother, grandmother and great-grand-mother; precisely who people are in the community, who and what their families were, where they live and where they used to live, are of vital importance. And they tell stories, constantly.

No one could ever mistake Jill McCorkle's Southern community for Eudora Welty's or Katherine Anne Porter's or Flannery O'Connor's. Yet neither could that particular community be thought of as existing anywhere but in North Carolina, in the South.

What the people in Miss McCorkle's fiction talk about, and seek again and again to come to terms with, is Change. Change, and its opposite and twin, Continuity. And it may well be that it is the impact of Change itself — social, political, economic, familial, racial — upon a society aspiring to permanence that has most of all characterized the Southern literary imagination. In Southern literature, things are always about to disappear.

For every Southern writer, apparently, there is in his or her experience the equivalent of the simultaneous existence of the Regency-Hyatt and the red-haired evangelist haranguing the quick and the dead on the corner by the Federal Building in Atlanta. Since that day eighteen years ago when my friends and I saw them, the Westin Peachtree (nee Peachtree Plaza) has introduced exposed, glass-enclosed elevator shafts far loftier than those of the Hyatt, and the evangelists appear to have taken to the television channels. Yet the contrasts within the Southern experience remain vivid, and the novelists still discover in them tensions. They have the urge to reconcile those tensions in the form of stories. That is what has created a lively and widely admired literature in the South, and that is what continues to expand that literature today. ■

VII.

And Lastly

Roy Blount Jr.

Raised in a prominent family in Decatur, Georgia, which clung to its small-town ways even as its younger neighbor Atlanta leaped toward urbanity, Roy Blount Jr. honed his talent by producing a humor column for the Decatur High Scribbler. *Scribbling ever since with a deftness that has brought him comparisons to W.C. Fields — not to mention H.L. Mencken and even Mark Twain — he earned degrees at Vanderbilt University and Harvard (the "Vanderbilt of the North") before becoming a reporter at* The Atlanta Journal, *where he stayed until* Sports Illustrated *beckoned. Since then, his essays, articles and stories have appeared in eighty-six different publications. Blount has become known not only as a prolific writer but also as a humorist-poet-performer-lecturer-dramatist on national radio, television and the New York stage, where he presented one-man shows in 1986 and 1988. Now, as you will read, he is about to add to his resume by becoming a presidential candidate. Blount lives in the North — in the heart of Manhattan — but says he feels more Southern there than in the South, a fact that might make him the perfect balanced ticket. If that sounds odd, even more offbeat comments fill his seven books, among them* Crackers, *which is being reissued with a new introduction in paperback in September. Blount's works have also appeared in forty anthologies.* ∎

The Next President
Of the United States

Well, when they said "brokered" and "somebody waiting in the wings," I never dreamed it would come around to where they meant me. And neither did they, I bet. For one thing, I figured I was part of "they." One of the ones sitting back looking down our noses at the candidates. I never thought for one minute, until recently, that I would be the one standing here looking down on everybody — humbly, but with pride.

True, I am a Democrat, in a high-minded kind of way, and then too, I grew up right outside of Atlanta here. So I know a little something about Southern politics, and I could see what the editors of *The New Republic* magazine were getting at when they wrote in their March 7 issue, "There is something special about the South. And it's not only that Democrats can't win without winning the South. . . . Who better than a reflective and articulate Southerner can speak about Union to and for a cynical and psychologically dismantled nation?"

But still. I mean, as of March 7, I hadn't popped up *at all*, in *any* of the polls.

But then Mike Dukakis let it slip that he couldn't really regard anybody as a true Democrat who wasn't Greek, and Richard Gephardt got carried away in a speech to the League of Women Voters and declared that he had always been a woman, and Paul Simon mysteriously took to wearing an ascot, and Tipper Gore — feeling defensive about charges that she had alienated the sixties generation — wrote a campaign song titled "Who Says He's Got to Stop Being Beaten by His Wife?" that had suggestive lyrics in it and then ran off with Twisted Sister, and Jesse Jackson was linked with Kurt Waldheim, and Bruce Babbitt turned out to be a Canadian national, and Gary Hart was photographed in bunny-foot pajamas with Jessica Hahn in *Playboy,* and Joe Biden, while speaking autobiographically to a labor group, lapsed into the lyrics (slightly adjusted) of "Coal Miner's Daughter," and Mario Cuomo came out with a book of meditations titled *I'd Rather Be Bright Than President,* and Bill Bradley had a midlife crisis and decided to forgo politics to try a comeback in the NBA, and Sam Nunn was revealed to have a brother in the warhead business who said he'd been raised to believe that capitalism meant being open-minded about who you do business with, and Ted Kennedy was endorsed by Richard Nixon, and Lee Iacocca was caught personally selling a used Chrysler with a Hyundai transmission in it at $1,200 over book value to a nun, and a stiff wind tumped the top three stories of Trump Tower over onto Fifth Avenue, and it came out that aides to Daniel Inouye had forcibly restrained him from slipping several million dollars for a Zoroastrian day-care center in Belgium into the budget bill (he confessed he couldn't stop himself; he had a craving to make weirdly inappropriate appropriations), and Warren Beatty completely lost his cool when asked about his Hart problem, and Bruce Springsteen said he wasn't really interested, and am I leaving anybody out?

Oh, and Oprah Winfrey and Phil Donahue had an actual knockdown, drag-out fight on *MacNeil-Lehrer,* and a computer was disclosed in Ted Koppel's hair, and Pat Schroeder got the giggles, and William Hurt cried, and Molly Ringwald turned out not to be old enough, and Henry Cisneros and several other up-and-coming young hopefuls said they wanted to wait until after the Depression started, and Gregory Peck said he wouldn't run unless he could dress up like Lincoln, and Ed Asner came over as too grumpy, and Kissin'

Jim Folsom turned out to be dead, and both Michael Jackson and Walter Cronkite said they weren't really interested. And Ed Koch was overheard remarking that he didn't like American food. And Mikhail Gorbachev said he wasn't really interested, but Raisa might be if the deal was right, which seemed a bit much.

Oh, and Walter Mondale said he was kind of tired, but he might like to be vice president again. And Jimmy Carter got his feelings hurt because it took so long before he figured in the speculation. And several other Kennedys were endorsed by Richard Nixon.

Well, even then I held back. I didn't want to be seen as thrusting myself forward, and my chief adviser — W.E. "Slick" Lawson of Nashville, Tennessee, author of the country song "I Won the Dance Contest Last Night But I Can't Take the Trophy Home" — agreed that that was wise, partly because he wanted to thrust himself forward.

So did several other of my articulate and reflective Southern friends. But while they were drinking and hollering, "You 'bout as reflective and articulate as a sick Dominecker chicken's breakfast" at one another, I was testing the waters.

I made a speech to the American Association of Businessmen Just About Barely Breaking Even What With the Way Things Are Going convention at Vail, Colorado. In that address, I put forward some of my common-sense economic proposals:

■ Reduce the federal deficit by citizen participation that is *bound*, if things add up at all, to pump money into the treasury without the government having to do anything hardly at all: Everybody go down to the post office and buy two rolls of stamps and throw them away.

■ Restore Wall Street to a sound foundation by requiring every securities transaction to be cash on the barrelhead, no bill larger than a twenty.

■ Make the dollar less silly by knocking the last digit off of every sum of money in America. Thus ballplayers would

236

make a hundred thousand dollars, the national debt would be down in the low hundred billions and a cup of coffee would be a nickel.

■ Restore the draft, not for young men but for corporate executives making over one million dollars a year including bonuses and weasel deals.

■ Explore the cost-effectiveness of putting able-bodied homeless persons through Outward Bound. (This was Slick's idea, and caused controversy, enabling me to show my toughness by firing him. I had already gotten out of him what I wanted, a campaign-song title: "I Will Treat You Like Your Momma Used to — Then Let's See 'Em Send Me Off to Jail.")

See, one thing a Southern articulate and reflective person feels it incumbent upon him to do is to be simple. You got to put the kibble over where the slow dogs can get some. I shouldn't be the one to say it, but these proposals gave me a Populist appeal.

Still I perceived that I was being perceived as too abstract and austere. A writer, not a politician. I knew enough about the Southern political tradition to realize that Ronald Reagan had mastered three important aspects of it *aside* from simple proposals:

1. Lying.
2. Easing folks' minds.
3. Setting an example of the feasibility of getting away with things.

I went to an image consultant. Told her I was just trying to gather material for my writing and asked her what if I had a friend who looked and sounded exactly like me but was too shy to come in himself? She prescribed a slight hitch in this friend's gitalong, which makes me less threatening and accentuates my homespunness, and also sold me an exact copy of the suit Jimmy Stewart wore in "Mr. Smith Goes to Washington," only colorized.

And before I knew it, I was carrying myself more Presidentially. A big media consultant came up to me on the street — didn't even know who I was — and said he had worked out a way through modern editing techniques to produce a TV spot of Will Rogers endorsing me.

"Won't the newspapers raise some questions about that?" I asked.

He said he had already fixed up a clip of Will Rogers saying, "All I know is what I see on the television."

But I didn't want to rely on electronic gimmickry. And I didn't want to focus on myself too much. That way I wouldn't have to be denying things all the time. The Reagan administration lost the people's trust because word got out that the Iran-contra thing was based on "plausible deniability." Here is how plausible deniability works:

When an administration is accused of something, its spokesman says, "Nothing could be further from the truth." In other words, "We don't see any way you can prove it, at least not for a while yet."

Then when evidence supporting the accusation comes out, the spokesman can say, "Well, some things could be further from the truth, but this is not at all the kind of thing we would do."

More evidence comes out. "Quite a few things could be further from the truth, maybe, but we could prove this isn't exactly the truth, if it weren't for national security reasons."

Irrefutable evidence comes out. "Well, let's say it is the truth. But we didn't know it was the truth."

Then, "At any rate, the president himself didn't know anything about it."

Then, finally, "There are no documents showing that the president ever told his wife. And we cannot comment on any further details because they are all subjects of litigation."

Somehow or another, in regard to the Iran-contra thing, this didn't go over. Maybe the Reagan administration should have taken a page from Jim Folsom, who took the position, "I always plead guilty." What a Southern politician might have said, right from the beginning, was, "We done it, and it

Roy Blount Jr. and Christabel King in their New York apartment.

On the roof of his Manhattan apartment stands humorist Blount, the unanimous next choice of the Democrats for president.

seemed like a good idea at the time, but them damn Iranians lied. Them damn Iranians can't be trusted any further than you can throw 'em, and I'd like to hear 'em deny it. But the deal looked like it would be good for a lot of loyal Americans and friends of America, and if you can't be loyal to your loyal American friends then what good are you?" I don't know whether that would have worked, but it couldn't have worked much worse than what the Reagan administration tried.

Still, the more I thought about this plausible deniability thing, the more I felt instinctively that the American people would go for it — the American people *like* plausibility — if somehow they could all be let in on it. So here's what I proposed, in a speech to the American Leeway Council. I proposed that the right to plausible deniability be extended to every American citizen.

Phone company calls up, says, "You haven't paid your bill in two months, and you owe us two-hundred and nineteen dollars."

You say, "Nothing could be further from the truth."

That confuses the phone company a little. "What do you mean by that?"

You say, "Well, I think my words speak for themselves."

Phone company: "Listen — all right, you have a telephone, right?"

"First I've heard of it," you say. "News to me."

The phone company gets excited: "*What do you mean, you don't know you have a telephone? We're talking to you on your telephone!*"

That's where you have to hang tough. You say, "That's your opinion."

And there are several different telephone companies out there in this great competitive land, so you've got some play.

Well, there is nothing Americans like better than some play. As one man, the American Leeway Council rose to give me a standing ovation — but I stayed them with a gesture and broke into the "Plausible Deniability Song":

Say you been cheating on your diet,
Or you went out and started a riot,
All you have to do is just ... deny it.
Deee-niability,
You don't have to have no humility,
If you've got de-ni-a-bil-i-ty.
And remember: You ... didn't hear it from me.

Well, "went over" is putting it mildly. If there's anybody who feels the burden of our being a debtor nation, it is the American Leeway Council. They whooped. They hollered. They carried me down to the marina proper and gave me a sixty-foot boat.

This was a crucial moment. The temptation was to rest on my laurels. But I saw that I was verging now on not being austere enough. So when interviewers came to me and asked about the bottom line, I said it was about time we opened the presidency to competitive bidding. And I came out with my ace-in-the-hole slogan:

"Just Pay Me What Ike Made."

Whoo, did interviewers' eyes light up. Even the ones who didn't want me to get away with it saw that I was golden.

"I believe I can get along," I said, "what with two nice free houses, city and country, on Ike's seventy-five thousand dollars."

Saves the nation a hundred and twenty-five thousand dollars a year right there. And reminds us of the fifties, which are coming back (if we keep our fingers crossed that it isn't the thirties), and of course, when you're invoking Ike, you're invoking bipartisan appeal. And you're offering balm to a long-festering old Southern resentment over the fact that, because of the Democratic Party, so many Southerners, or anyway their parents, found themselves voting for Adlai Stevenson.

And the next thing I knew, the phone rang and it was old Bob Strauss saying, "I bleeve Scooter it is time for you and me to sit down with a few of the boys."

And here I am. I thank you for the nomination. And if I

have come this far this fast over every other Democrat in America, I don't see why I can't whip one measly wore-out Republican.

(Prolonged demonstration on the floor.)

And I pledge this to you:

When I am elected, I will honor the office by staying in it. Out of America's way. Ronald Reagan has already demonstrated that the president who seems to get the most things done is the president who lets things go.

He was good at that because he was an actor. I'll be good at it because I'm a writer. Four years at seventy-five thousand dollars per is a heck of a book advance. I'll bet three-fourths of Southern literature was produced for less than three hundred thousand dollars, all together. I'm going to *write* my presidency. And you won't have to worry about how I'm doing till the book comes out, in the fall of 1992.

Then I will go on my promotion tour — also my re-election campaign. And the talk-show hosts will flip through my five hundred-odd pages of solid accomplishment and ask me, "Are you sure you didn't just make this up?"

And I will say, "Nothing could be further from the truth." ∎

About the Editor

Dudley Clendinen, the editor of this collection, was born in Tampa, Florida, in August 1944, to a journalistic family that has inhabited the South for more than two hundred years and embraced both sides of the Civil War. Educated at Vanderbilt University, he joined the *St. Petersburg* (Florida) *Times* in 1968 and ranged across the lower South as an investigative reporter and columnist for that paper for most of the seventies. His conflict-of-interest reporting led to the U.S. House of Representatives' reprimand of former Representative Bob Sikes, dean of the Florida delegation, in 1976. As a metropolitan reporter in New York and then national correspondent for *The New York Times* in Boston and Atlanta, he covered issues ranging from Love Canal to AIDS, acid rain, civil rights affairs, the trials of Jean Harris and Claus von Bulow, the selling of U.S. Navy secrets by the Walker spy family, the 1984 presidential campaign and the effects of drought and the economy on the culture of the rural South. He has reported on five national political conventions and is now assistant managing editor for features of *The Atlanta Journal* and *The Atlanta Constitution.* He is the author of the text for a book of photographs, *Homeless in America,* published by Acropolis Books in Washington, D.C., earlier this year.

About the Photographer

During a four-month project that covered nearly twenty thousand miles and eight states, staff photographer Andy Sharp visited the seventeen authors in this collection at their homes to capture their character on film. A photographer at The Atlanta Journal-Constitution since 1980, Sharp lives in Marietta with his wife, Jody, and two children, Austin and Amanda.

ACKNOWLEDGMENTS

The writers published here offer a wonderful array, and I am grateful to them for their writing and rewriting, for their strong early interest in the project and for their persistence in seeing it through. Seventeen authors do not fall all at once into the form of a book. All of these had other writing and teaching projects. A number of them wrote several drafts as this collection developed. Several were on deadline for their own books. One, Alex Haley, finally found the time on the far side of several midnights, in the painful quiet of a hospital bed in Knoxville, Tennessee. But this collection of their work is also the product of the collective effort of a number of other writers and editors and artists at *The Atlanta Journal* and *The Atlanta Constitution.* We are indebted to them, and I would like to thank them here. Mary Ellen Pettigrew, as senior editor, coordinated the growth of this project over many months, seeing to everything. Michael Carlton, Mary Lee, Mary Alma Welch and Ralph Patrick read and re-read, edited and re-edited the essays as the collection grew. Andy Sharp took all the photographs. Keith Graham wrote the biographical sketches and much of the captions for the photographs. Marchant Roach and Lillian King were invaluable editorial assistants in the production process. Van McKenzie, Rick Jaffe and Al Levine designed the magazine in which the essays originally appeared. Under the direction of Earl Batton, Bill Lambert, Richard Walker, William Willoughby and David Powell, the composing and platemaking departments of the paper put the words, pictures and art elements to paper with precision. It was a pleasure. ∎